# camping underground

# camping underground

## Greg McLaren

PUNCHER & WATTMANN

First published in 2022
Published by Puncher and Wattmann
PO Box 279
Waratah NSW 2298

https://www.puncherandwattmann.com
web@puncherandwattmann.com

ISBN    9781922571502

Cover design by David Musgrave and Greg McLaren
Typesetting by Morgan Arnett
Printed by Lightning Source International

A catalogue record for this work is available from the National Library of Australia

NATIONAL
LIBRARY
OF AUSTRALIA

*They developed a taste for ruined houses, and for ghosts.*

Randolph Stow, *The Merry Go Round in the Sea*

*If you can't win the game, then don't lose the fight.*

Terry Butler

## "camping underground"

*After.*

Darl, when it began
I thought I was prepared –

I'd been watching *The Walking Dead.*

*After.*

Grass thrives in the ghosts of cars in front yards.
Well, of course
                        it does.
Engine blocks blossom.

*Just before.*

On the socials and all that,
lots about the first few in that series of bombings –
how *a very friendly man* had asked
another passenger to mind his bag/backpack/
suitcase while he *ducked to the loo.*

Just a small, very targeted blast. Only one
or two victims, maybe selected, maybe
random – a woman on the Sutherland line, a Malay
Muslim lady just out of Granville, and

a French backpacker at Circular Quay,
two retired State level cricketers at Strathfield.
Someone said it sounded *like a hammer dropped on a tin roof.*


*After.*

Long strips of broken shade spill across Vincent Street –
a dismantled piano keyboard.
                                    The wind through those gaps
is a heated, repeated tune.


*Getting out.*

There's a woman, 7.23, in the doorway
of her art deco flat the next floor up
in a brown-looking dressing gown, choking a longneck,
a.m.


*After. Rain, now.*

's warmer and more frequent. There's
a hard and pointed glare it slicks on
to even the grimiest surface,
on everything, after its nightful of water –

the cracked concrete slabs, leaves, dirt trails,
roads, what used to be lawns, the wear-torn
duco of cars, that pair of skinny jeans
encasing a femur.


*After.*

The small town
at the south-east edge of what'd
seemed
      safe —

the neat array of bodies in front yards:
feet first, entry wounds clean
in their foreheads.

And, looking closer — you always
need to look closer — small
marks pocked in the skin,

like a speed limit sign
dinged with pellets
from a moving car

or a ute.

*After.*

Livestock started showing up everywhere, and dogs.
Now, I travel in the dark with cows,
                                        but just
inside the tree line.
You have to develop an attitude.


*Before. Who let the bugs out? Woof woof, etc.*

A source close to the research clinic
suggested the behaviour was not
what had been evident

in the modelling
or the laboratory.
On the autofeed,

she's weeping:
*The engineering process, this is*
*not what we would have expected,*

*this was not the intended*
*application* (meaning,
not here). She coughs,

shoots herself.
The focus fixed on her chin,
the seeping muck.

*After. Adding the 't'.*

*Auburnt*, he said, with a hiccup or a tremor.
*And the oval was bloody well rank with headscarves.*

*Weeks before. Dry run.*

Everyone at Cronulla North that Australia Day
got sick –
            terrible runs and a bad flu. The rash.

*After.*

Black-shouldered kite
orbits a spot above the fire trail
then drops
            on the sharp-hinged air.
Get off the path.
                Quick.
                        Down.
Is it someone, dead?
Or alive, which could be worse.

*Then – right then.*

The first I heard – I thought I heard – was
a rash of fireworks near the racecourse.
The sound of yelling, more bungers, then silence,
except for the sound of running/stopping/hiding.

Something sparks in, or against,
the night's damp gauze –
                              a neighbour
in the next lot rubbing a switch,
an image skidding from a dream.

Wouldn't've done that.
Someone at their door.

Two days later, his head out in the hot street –
his face, featureless
                              as a country airport.
Apart from the flies, that is.

It had been said he had a "vernacular way" of playing footy.

*Before.*

That last PM
and his anti-gay agenda –

who does he think
designed those suits?

*Then.*

*Kate! Where u?*
*U OK?*

No reply.
Then the reports online,
and I know.

My texts stall in the air.

*Then. Ish.*

Then one day, the network went down
and stayed down.
Things looked bad.

*After.*

Along the railway
from stanchions,

the council of developers,
the miners' government

dangle buzzed and charred,
hooked up as bait

for who was left
 from the military,
 the local muscle,
 their families.

Word still got around
    for a while.


*After.*

Overnight a downpour of dog spoor, two dozen
or more. I set a trail for the dogs into the nuts and guts
of the camp I'm watching. I'm not talking puppies here.
Long gone feral, with an influx from Bellbird's
loosed rotties and staffies.
      It takes a long time to go quiet.
I'm not proud but I'm glad.
      As a kid I'd wiggle a stick
or length of choko vine into cinder blocks or gaps
between bricks,
   into the mess of webs redbacks make,
tease the spiders out, and an inch from my fingers,
sling them into the jar,
    because.

*After.*

Two years, three years – who knows.
New detachments dither up the valley roads
at last, calling us out. Decontamination showers
and out before dawn from these ringed-in compounds.

On the train to who knows – between tight
irregular trees, the sun spreads from below
the horizon onto the clouds' fresh undersides
along a slim and flickering burning band,

the reddest thing, apart from children's exposed intestines,
I ever saw –
                garrotte-thin at first,
the first still from a thermonuclear blast.

Then I wake.


*Before.*

A child, from ballet class, called Sofala.


*Before. T-shirt. (They were onto something).*

Happy virus

*Then.*

Someone says they saw
       three guys in hi-vis vests
       slung with AKs
              and a belt
of sweating canisters they unscrewed,
which started to hiss.

Then a heap of people
              choking,
coughing – the fumes.
The sound of shooting, maybe,
from out of frame.

In the scale of things,
it was hardly blankets snug with smallpox
or strychnine in the vittles,
                   but,
still.
There were stacks of clips like this
until the links broke again and stayed broke.

*Before.*

I used to go posting photos on tumblr
of consecutively numbered houses
in runs of 100.

What else was there to do?

*After.*

Lakemba mosque, filled with
Syrian and Sudanese Christians offered refuge –
locked in and lit as someone's idea
of, what, retaliation? But aren't they all about
                                    god?
Blokes in Aussie flag burqas, toting kero tins,
ex-army issue weapons
at a very specific location,
                    not for the first time.
*This is concerning*: the PM's response.


*After.*

A half-burnt body
with a Long Bay blue southern cross
neck tattoo.


*After.*

The drains around Cessnock were spongy with maggots,
a smoke of flies. People got sloppy in the panic, of course:
death and attrition, boredom in the landscape of rivals –

in the park, emergency refuge at the start, now slippery with dead –
ibises, only five of them, gorged,
incapable of flight. Meaning, *Hello, dinner.*

And I used to be a vego.

*After.*

Every now and then
              you look up.
                          Today the cumulus flap
and roll, flap and roll, slowly,
                    folded deep into some future.


*After.*

*Camping underground*, that
was the saying, the euphemism, in the forward knots of quick huts
on high ground, in the first string of towns around here
that held together.
                        Then someone got that phrase and took it
literally:
              snipers on the roof of the Neath Hotel
as the families sheltered in the damp galleries
of the ancient colliery,
                    picking off the others as they came through,
that surly column of bikes.


*After.*

Shit.
     That red dress,
              its black butterfly motif,
clasping her breasts.

             Her breasts.

*A long while after. These binoculars are pretty good.*

This squad of guys, moving as one –
each one built like a brick shithouse,
each one's head shaved, or maybe scalded, and tattooed

like gaol tatts, blue-green – circles inside
circles, over a kind of grid, over their whole
forehead.
              Real intricate shit.
                          It's up of two years
since but their weapons look new.

Barrels and blades glint like a new logo,
the light off them blunt as a train.

*After.*

Glad I kept some old skills fresh
                         orienting by sight
and memory.
Thanks, Brown Owl.

No google maps, no live traffic feed.

*After.*

It's like at the movies – *Look out! behind you!*

*After.*

The country we thought we knew
is gone. But its harbour-mouthed rivers
still drain from the steady low mountains.

Exclusion zones and quarantined towns
are busy with grass, now, spread wide
as cattle ribs right through that long drought.

Tall lights scan perimeters at the old showground –
wind-blown blossoms, spot fires –
and sirens spin through the night like alarmed plovers.

It's hard to get through to people, still.


*After. I loaded the dog.*

The idea was to snag one of their dogs,
load it with semtex, send it on home. Good boy!

Getting the timer to work
was the trick, though, but it did.

I don't know why
you wouldn't believe in the redemptive

power of literature, or doubt
its real-world applications.

*After.*

The chemists emptied quick
but in one, at the Pharmacist Advice counter –

## Tarot Reader
## On Monday Book Now


*Before.*

A shoe in the road,
turned on its side.
Someone at the top
of the hill.
        Just
like that.


*After. Birds.*

The ravens are scolding
something beyond the tree line
past the fence.
        A snake, probably,
egg-hungry, a goanna, or a couple
of the devils scouring village corpses
all directions out from the Tops –
at night you hear them, they tear air
from their throats and bicker full-
throttle over a scrap, crunch up bones

loud as.

    Then, from in there, a thud and
two voices. Rattle
a few guns,

        two more mines go off.
Three men, boys, more like,
patches of grass on their hats, rise
as one and move, careful:
two shots almost muffled
in the dirt, and quiet.

        That's
a good use for birds.


Is it that crew from Maitland? Getting
ahead of themselves, aren't they?



*Dreaming, years before.*


We don't wake
but dream of smoke
thick as a dusty gag – there,
an image of my daughter:


but I don't have a daughter.


Why is she so tall there,
on the flashing brilliant lawn,
waiting? The open doorway
hisses,

    the night so bright
and enormous.

*After, before, could be either. But after. You guessed that.*

Past Telarah, stalled, a coal train –
a long black necklace ready
to be clasped.


*Before. Lucas Heights.*

The truck bomb at Lucas Heights
was a feint,
           the clever stupid bastards
just as the AFP went into Kirribilli House.
Another squad of Blue Cross went in
as the Mack went up, wearing burqas.
They blew the shit out of the reactor
and left only their shaky live feed
and a bloated ellipse of suburbs dusted
by the unexpected southerly.
The thefts from oncology departments
at RPA and John Hunter: that was them too,
so they said – that stuff found its way
into dirty bombs along the eastern seaboard
those long three days after.
Before, they couldn't agree on a thing,
turned up at the wrong pubs.
                      Who the fuck
has fed those clowns some brains for once?

*After, but not long.*

Stragglers up from Sydney –
some with sores from the radiation,
others hot and sniffling
with the first visible signs of the bug.
What were we supposed to do?


*After.*

The Bolwarra organic farmers
and vegans were the ones we thought would be the first
to go under,

but their organisational capacity
was really something –

keeping their anarcho-syndicalist commune
afloat and warning off the hardest nuts
in the last shreds of bike gangs.

I would not call them gentle.


*Before, on the way to Maitland.*

Why shouldn't a woman in a headscarf
be reading Matthew Reilly on the train?

*Before.*

A local clip; not the first incident
around here, but the footage
gone viral 0 to 60:

Broadmeadow station,
the bridge's shade on its slow
creep along the platform.

There're two men, moving erratically,
torsos hovering above the kids
squatting/standing, arsing about –
first day of the Show.

A woman edges back,
draws two children behind her,
and is screaming,

*No, put it down, no. Oh, fuck no.*

White noise white space.

Then the awning's underside, motionless.

*Before. Still life with still-birth.*

The vase on the trundle table –
flowers, natives sent by friends
assuming, and wishing the three of us,
the best.
       The empty ward of light
falls across them.
             The midwife
unable to find a heartbeat.
                 So,
of wattlebird feathers
that remind me of those thin
pale striations
in orange tree flesh

caught in the low
winter morning sun
that trickles between
the shed and the flats
behind
       as our daughter
plays in her toy car
and rolls herself in dew:

so,
    none of that.

But.
    *The first time
ever I saw your face.*

*Before. What did I have against you?*

What do I have
             against you?
                          Mum, are you fucking serious?
You left me with Grandad all week.
Didn't you notice?

You know what he's like.
                          I saw you.

*After.*

Inside the house,
and the rug, you notice
straight off, 's
disturbed, not aligned,
the way the rest
of the room is —
the dresser, the IKEA
shelving (is that Kallax?),
the double bed, somehow,
still looks just-made,
the off-white top sheet
turned over and smoothed-out.
Under the rug
the floor gives a bit, and,
jemmied up, the boards
lift and dust rises
in from the dark recess below.
Some smart bastard

with a short run of luck –
no bolt house, but a stash:
case after case
of oxycodone and one
box of generic brand amoxycillin:
but first, wipe off that icing
of cockroach turds.


*After.*

You learn, approaching towns,
camps, settlements, whatever
whoever calls them, to go calm
and listen hard for birds – grounded

plovers, ravens, the Torresian crows
drifting further south each quick
breeding season. They'll rise
and snark you out as you get too near.

And, probably, you'll die, and die slowly.


*Right then? Was this it?*

"Trying to get out north, we
were stopped, not searched.
Maybe scanned or assessed.

The sticking heat, the wind
beginning, in gusts, the punters
nervy, the soldiers clearly pissed off,

twitchy, getting bored, probably
wanting to get home. A voice crackles
from the shoulder mic on an NCO.

She frowns and makes a white question
from her face. *I want to go,*
I say to him, *We better go right now,* so we go,

unrushed but quick, out of that weather —
the storm really was hurrying in.
Roll away past the crowd,

careful of the people lined up
and on foot. The lightning starts cracking out
from over the ranges, and then,

back on the tar, as we're heading away,
I hear this hard clacking
that sounds not that much

like thunder. Like really angry typing".
Or so she said. I don't know. It seems a bit
rehearsed — I reckon she knows more.

*After.*

The vegans loved it when the Patriots
appeared at the gates, sick,
malnourished, up from the river, sores
all over their faces. *You cunts*
*can't be asking for* refuge,
*can you? You aren't, are you,*

*snowflake?*


*After.*

No more deadshits
dawdling on their phones —
that has to be a plus.


*After.*

Bell mynahs ring back
from the dementia terror makes —

a sonar depth sounding.


*After.*

I'm on prehistoric Stella and ancient augmentin
for my sinus this spring, barely out of bed

all week, backing up the eyes we keep
out at Laguna, watching for our friends
from the Macdonald Valley.
Someone
came in off a side-track, run out of food.
Two women, a boy. We took them in a day,
let them clean up and wash their hair.


*After.*

In those rooms and halls,
the smell of piss, blood, semen,
long after the women've been
moved.


*After. What he said.*

Finn says, *Nice to have you here.*
*We just have to ride this*
*out. Everyone here works,*
*long as they can. What is it*
*you do?*
I ask for paper,
write a list.
His eyebrows
kind of arch, almost comically,
so I guess he's covering
for his eyes, the corners
of his mouth.

*After.*

Out scouting into the Wollemi,
just in case. The only thing moving
is clouds. There's nothing much in here
for the devils, but we saw their work,
once —
        a body upside down in a tree,
ankle-pinned, and the head, which the devils
could reach, gone, the shoulders
pretty-well chewed-at. At a stream we strip
and wash. In the water our faces
are submerged by new features —
gravity's gotten at my body already.

*Before.*

It's hard to say who'd bought-off
the AFP, if that's what even happened.
When they took The Lodge and Kirribilli House
the same morning, and found not
the PM but his deputy, the full Aaron
Sherritt, found under his bed — holes
everywhere,
                they said.

*After.*

We pick up some stuff on the radio
now, excerpted through the shit generators we use.
Maybe it will be all over soon,
                              or eventually.
The sun clatters through clouds
above our small crises – a bung flue, a shit harvest,
the army and something else maybe, building
out past the Golden Highway: says the talk coming in,
in its dribs and drabs. That could
                              be a good thing,
depending on who, depending on who for.


*After.*

Summer nearly done, the long
summer. Nearly May, if
we've reckoned right, and the rising
steam from drying mud in the old
wetlands is a rich and fertile thing,
accompanied by smokes of mosquitoes
lifting even in the dry districts and fecund
with Ross River, encephalitis and the first stings,
we think, of malaria.

*After.*

With the plague
the end came
with violent sneezes

and coughing – dark sprays
of snot like supernovas.
I saw the spread

graphed out once,
some funky infographic
days before it really

took off, mapped onto space
with small dots
coloured to denote

the rising intensity of infection,
its virulence – a spatter
of data, a kid's picture

of what the stars
might look like.
That's

when we started
to avoid company, and
fairly assiduously at that.

But then the vigils.

*Before.*

My sister, two weeks
after she took out finance
to replace her old Lancer,

had her temp role go under
and landed on the streets in Brisbane,
which is where I found her

to bring home to mum
and what's his name in that hot
little house at Windale he'd inherited.

That's when she saw Ridley,
and kept seeing him. I guess.

      *"Seeing"*.

*Before.*

That last squelch of short-lived
Liberal PMs shored up
their positions, their slim margins
the only thing modest about them.

*After.*

DIRT DIRT DIRT

*During.*

Quarantined. The whole country.
Except Christmas Island.
Ha.
    Ha.
Sad because it's true.
Funny, too, because, it's true.


*Getting out.*

The main roads blocked or gone – remembering
side paths onto the old fire trails from Guides,
and up the hills' steep and gullied
switchbacks, gunning the car up through there

there and over, walking the rest
of the way, past the party bus, empty,
headed once for the vineyards, and must've
detoured and detoured one of those early

nights: the doors swinging out and draining
dew onto the wrong side of the road –
look, a Louis Vitton handbag squeezed

behind the left rear tyre, unzipped.
a sharded compact's sticking out,
catching a crack of the sun. That happened, too.

She said.

*After.*

The paths into Newcastle always
shifting, making new maps
in our heads, using the old ones
as overlays – sinkholes, sent up
from collapsed mines after tremors,
after a decent rain, no maintenance, or
for no reason you could see.
                    From where
the cathedral used to be,
you could make out the  bits of depressed trails
convicts and their descendants had made
under the ground, dragging coal out in buckets,
black as the forgetting the town
tried to do, dark and shaded
as the forgetting we worked at,
and what would come
                    later, after.


*After.*

There's a rabbit in the grass,
upright, looking into the cover.

Me, I'm watching for the hawk.

*After.*

The vineyards were a fucking mess.
That was the best security they could buy?


*After.*

The field hospital. Early days. What
was left of the cops thought they had
the epidemiology down. High temps

for three days meant it was about to spread.
People were already gun-happy,
as if it was a means of control

where there was none.
                              *But you can*
*see he has an infection. Look at his arm.*

*He isn't sick. You can't.*
                              But he could and he did.
*You just can't.*
                    What was there, then,
that wasn't too late?


*Before.*

The new low-tech thing is pushing people into the paths of trains.
Hard not to take that personally.

*Before.*

Carpet re-zoning of slabs of suburbs for high-density —
investors and developers loved it, and the recipients
of their largesse in parliaments and council chambers.
Though the plebs shunted further out, or who had homes
acquired, were less than keen.

This bug, this plague, its long trails

of carcass, its variable genetics, yep, it fucken well
loved that shit. So thanks,

thanks a lot.

*After.*

The virus moving, a predator rippling out across the flat
and crowded suburbs, the busy districts,
following the movement of crowds, — it loved
an audience — speeding into dense populations,
a whale slicing through dark and silent water
after cornered schools, slurping us up like krill.

*After.*

YEAH GET UP

*After.*

Autumn at last –
cockatoos strip out
the mandarin orchard,

preferring the early
bitterer fruit.

*After.*

Car bombs are so Julia Roberts,
circa 1993, *The Pelican Brief,* but then,
I am a legal romcom kind of girl.

*After.*

Dear Ruthie, dear
you, where do I put
all these bits and pieces?
Do I assemble them,
or do you, if we ever
find you. I want you
to know everything,
or some of it.
You know what I'm not
saying, don't you?

*After.*


Praise. Some folks here have still
got god, and they're full of it —
praise. They praise the events
and people that brought us here;
they praise the crows, the light
slack on their feathers; the ants
that strip and polish everything
that falls (everything falling);
the potholed roads that tear
away into places we no longer
know; they praise the M16s
we fell upon; the high ground
here with hills at its back; the deep
stream and strip of wetland
beyond; it seems to do them
good, or some good. I can't believe,
but the praising can't hurt, can it?
So I might as well.
            No, actually,
screw it.


*Before.*


Dirty bomb in the maternity tent
of the internment camp.
Another clip
        of kids' feet
poking out from under tarps.

*After. On Country.*

Aunty Kez smiles her kind-of smile.
I return it.
> *Come on in.*
> *It's been hard on you, hasn't it?*
Nod, it's all I can do —
*hard* is the least of it, and one thing
I know is I don't need to tell her that.
> *If you're ready to listen, love,*
> *take a seat.*
There was only the one.
I take it, and nod.
> *This Country,*
she begins.


*Before.*

Government websites cloned
as .gov.fu


*After. Getting out.*

Crossing the creek at night,
full moon.
That was my mistake, going
along with that plan. Someone's child
clinging to my back.

                    And, the way
it always happens, the shooting starts.
A warm feeling everywhere, but
no pain, only a slackness I didn't
want to name.
                    Don't
                              make me
tell you. Please,
                    don't.


*Before. You'd think.*


Protests – it loved
the protests against the lock-in,
and the vigils, and the rest.
You'd think we'd learn.


*Before. As a consequence.*


The children of the environment minister
had vanished. It was highly orchestrated –

they were found floating off the reef,
doused with bleach,
tattooed with *Daddy.*

They never spoke.

*After.*

Once a backyard goey enthusiast,
now a sentry-cum-sniper-cum-whatever.

Somewhere, there's singing, more
or less.
            The next thing, her top
was coming off over her head,
sliding from her shoulders, those
wiry arms.
            My mouth sudden
on her mouth. Her hand
at my vulva.



*After.*

Cessnock. Where else
would you stage
the end of the world?



*Before.*

I remember our last time
in that hot dusty house
the pink fibro, the floors we swayed on;
streaming Nina Simone on Spotify,
The Beasts of Bourbon left on
in the spare room as we fucked

and fucked on the table
to Brian Hooper's foxy basslines.


*After. Neoliberal economics.*

There was time just enough
to clean out the shops once
before the supply chains turned cactus.


*Before.*

The parents fought. Didn't
everyone's? Oh. It was the fucking
or the betting or the wanting the other
to be hopelessly wrong.

And then mum would slide
the keys across the laminex counter,
that sound like the start

of a piss, or a knife
sharpener, and into the car and off
she'd go, off into the afternoon,
the weekend sour and awful

as our runny nervous shits. And dad,
silent to us after, faceless
as if stilling his thousand voices until

she rang to not speak but to
deliver some blunted
rhetorical force: *I can.* But I never
especially liked drugs or the drinking

my sister did, my brother. I just
broke off into small portions and
let them slowly heal, or not,

and I tipped into walking and finding
what was wherever, always ready
to just go. Not actually wanting
to, mind, but ready.


*Before.*

Kiribati became a reef
and we stopped the boats.


*After.*

The plague's, we decided, tidal, running now
on a long wash in — there's something

about or in these new summers: the numbers lift
and float out, unmoored.
Autumn hauls back in, and,

as the maples turn, infections
fall to next to nothing. Red leaves,

orange leaves, littered seed pods
from turpentines — the index
of recovery.


*Before.*


The custard pie the former Home Affairs
Minister bought in the face
at his final presser,
making everything official at last —
laced with arsenic.
                    The gasping,
the waggling cameras and the actual
falling and dying. Nobody sure what to do.
No-one minded, not really.


*Before. Where Ridley went.*


Kids tie off in storm drains,
slant light,
hugging a goon.

That's where he went,
I think.
        He never said
what had happened to him,

did he?

*Before.*

Lorikeets, little iridescent Geiger counters
in the ironbark.


*Before.*

For a few days the phones
in the pockets and bags of the dead
kept on buzzing and ringing –

the array of tones,
the water, the sky and trees
all wild with light.


*Before. Gold Sing Australian and Chinese Family Restaurant.*

A sheet of glass
on the Chinese takeaway's counter,
flattening the menu
like a slide sample.

The early evening light
seeps through
the curtained door.
A middle-aged couple,

arrive with their own
cutlery and plates,

take their seat
next to the cork landscape,

its reflection cased in glass.
The sound from the kitchen
of spring rolls in the fryer –
bathwater running.

That jangling – is it
the change in the waiter's pockets,
or the dusty brass bell
over the doorway?

Back to the dishes for me,
funding what passes for an education.


*After.*

Shopping trolleys make a weir across the river.


*After.*

Wandering cows; the grass man-high;
fence wire to trip on's still snaking with rust;
a horse, wholly disarticulated; that old
crush, irreparable.
                    This paddock's a field of nouns.
The past is an artesian bore.

*Before.*

The waiting room. In this one,
waiting on the verdict

on the angry spot above my right tit,
Billy Joel smacks out the closing chords to *Piano Man.*

It gets worse – Lou Gramm lip-syncs
*I've been waiting for a girl like you*
*to come into my life.*


*Public transport scam, overheard twice. Before. Der.*

*Listen, this is on vibrate.*
*I can't talk, not really.*
*It's done, Michelle and Lisa*
*put it on the internet*
*two and a half hours ago.*
*No, it's done, there's nothing*
*to be done, just wait.*
*I've been on the phone to Qantas,*
*there are no seats left,*
*only a thing they have called reserve.*
*If a spot comes up, they call you,*
*but I'm $98 short,*
*I don't start work until next*
*Monday, I don't know a soul*
*over here. No, I've already knocked*
*on three church doors.*
*No, I'll just have to give it up*

*and hope the universe*
*will come through for me.*
*I'm heading to what they call Central,*
*I just need somewhere noisy,*
*with lots of people around,*
*and wait.*
                    *But they haven't*
*heard the last of this.*
*Out of respect for mum*
*I'll wait a while, but no*
*Australian should have to put up*
*with this. Excuse me,*
*I just had to blow my nose.*
*Yeah, I'll see ya.*

Some sucker turns and leans into him
with a kind frown and a twenty.

*After. First camp: why I couldn't stay.*

Someone in the waking
clammy night began
shrieking out prophecies

in the voice, it seemed,
of a child. Fairly reasonable
predictions, you'd think –

fires tearing up the mountains,
sick people running,
ash everywhere,

ash shaped like people,
*The bad men are coming for us.*
It just went on

until there was a quiet snap.
In the morning I took
maybe a minute to see

who wasn't there anymore.
Sometimes I can't stand
to be around people.

So I went,
                without a word.


*After.*

The clouds, their small
crackling fissures of light –
opening like an ice sheet.


*After.*

On patrol where those dickhead Cullen twins
once lived, I keyed a whole rash of cars
along their old street, hoping, hopelessly
lost in a reverie of revenge and nostalgia.

*After.*

Remnant stands of the old scrub are coming back,
springing out from rail corridors and the parks system,
bedded under with slips of fern,
fulfilling the promise of work for the dole bush regen.

*After.*

Despite it all,
the wattlebirds still sound
like a car trying to turn over.

*After.*

Early on, the grain silos
were drained, once it got realised
things really had changed.

From one, near Bolwarra,
they said, slid two kids –
in her fist a frayed wish of rope.

*Before. No means.*

*I just couldn't believe he kept asking me.*

*Mutineers. After.*

Sun speckled and glinting all along the beach's golden slit.
Warm, maybe even hot, with breeze enough.

Amnesty Week, reps from all around, peaceable –
the local crews settling down at last, finally
dropping the constant muscle, the jumps,

the dopey waste. Towards Nobby's the stiff breakers
fall across the breakwater's last thin strand, flashing

spittle and foam into the gob of the poor
portless river. To Bar Beach? Burwood?

*No, isn't Merewether's too far? – got to get back*

*to the curfew zone by dark.* South end
of Newcastle, below the damp ferny drop spilling

a cool tongue down almost to the tidal
fringe, smoke of birds, the disputing ravens and
gulls wild and in at something, a whale calf,

or some useful thing. Staked into the sand,
three sets of legs and arms busted, at wrong angles,

three bodies stripped and left there:
lips pouting like stranded anemones, small fish
kissing at the faces, slippery beaks clacking

at the eye-flesh and -lids, the birds turning
for a second to the fresh fruit of my spew

even while I try to keep a lid on that joke –
what do you call a man with no arms
or legs in the pool? Bob –

as she pulls me away, her eyes silent
and bolting, stuck to the cliff-line and

we stumble away from that quick-spoiling flare,
someone's signal to someone, a pall, guessing
what it was.


*Before.*

When Ridley
published his book –

not the thing he stapled together
in his teens,
but *The Golden Highway* –

the Advertiser's page eleven headline
might as well have read:

LOCAL MAN WRITES POEMS:
ISN'T A COMPLETE POOF

*Before.*

It's not big-noting myself
but the car bombs, the stabbings,
I never gave that much of a shit.
On the platforms and on the concourses,
on the train and at the shops,
I'm watchful. I keep almost
to myself.
                How easy and happy
people were to give in,
as if the world weren't bloodily earnt.
Panic?
            I wish they fucking
had.
            The Patriots scared
the living shit out of me –
I knew them.
                So when that
first packet of dirty bombs went off like
a weekend at schoolies,
                            I knew
something was on its way out.
                            The virus hit,
slow at first, after the hospital shootings, one
small light
                winking out at a time, like a night
slipping in
                over the mountains when you're a kid,
the light washed-out looking, impossibly
far.
        Even from the far end, looking down
into the valley from what looks

like safety,
            the day still peels so quick away,
over the rises and the drops,
                        the trees'
darkening canopies and the small,
isolated houses way out
                        from anywhere you know
and that you'll head for one day,
hooning like a bastard.



*Before/After. Thinking about Kate.*


Laying with you,
talking,
the music left on from before —

PJ Harvey wants Robert
de Niro to sit on her face.
You nominate Dorothy Porter

but mean Dorothy Parker
probably. Even through
the speaking our slippery

fingers do, I can't
say your name now, or not
the way I want to,

thinking how it was —
flashing Venus
climbing down our long

and watchful sky.
Your whole skin still –
an early morning river.


*After.*

The unfinished apartments – the slots
in the brick wall for letterboxes look ready
for crematorium memorial plaques.


*Before.*

My sister spent years living in hallways,
always near the coal line.

My attitude to family
was never what it could have been.

But no wonder.


*Foraminifera field work. Before.*

Long hours.
The sunburn,
the chafing,
the chapped lips,
the numb feet,

cramped thighs,
the slow burn on your eyes.
Hard on the knees.
Repeat.
But I love it,
the plotting out of tiny
points of data,
fragment by fragment,
scrapping and peeling away
each speck of sun-denied sand
at a time,
telling us barely anything
about the fossil weather –
meaning the long tides
and silting of climate
that went on and goes on
somewhere almost forever.
Oh, and the coffee is rubbish
unless you bring your own pot.


*Before. Research.*


Yep, the papers
that eleven people
would read.
Those tiny shells,
small traces
of large consequence.

*Before.*

Kate's fibroids.


*Before. Bugged. Lol.*

Soft clicks on the line
and then he'd need a nervous
quick durry outside.


*After.*

If this is Gilligan's Island
(what one of the oldies call us),
then I bags Mary-Ann.


*After.*

I think the worst thing
I saw was a collapsible pram
writhing in the running gully.

*After.*

Deep in the woods
I smell her patchouli (yes, srsly)
just before the low voices.


*Before.*

Exactly when did asking Christian
religious leaders to address the radicalisation
and extremism in their communities

begin to sound like satire?


*After.*

Front yard boats fill with rain, and breed mosquitoes.


*After.*

I slip off my mask, and he says,
*Shit, he's a chick.*
And pulls a blade, and that's when
I have to kick his head in.

Like, literally.

*After. Hawkers.*

Camp to camp, town
to barricaded town, for a while,
posing convivial threats if not
humoured
            or watched close enough.
The faces change,
there's a rich turnover as
their businesses get *acquired*
on the roads between.
The stuff they bring's seasonal.
So we let it be known
on the quiet what we need,
and the info they share's sensitive
but carefully non-vital. When, or if,
we all start to get together
again from our little local
seats of power, becoming all municipal again,
these guys will have to go –
because
            of what they know.
                                        Sorry.


*Before.*

The big girl, freckled,
her black t-shirt:
*Maybe if this shirt is witty*
*enough, someone*
*will love me.*

I smiled and tried,
but never did.


*Before.*

The gunman was lost in the hotel
so she called the lobby for help.


*After.*

Our patrols worked in twos
and I was matched up with the hopeless newbie.

I was impaired.


*Before. At least he said he did.*

Ridley so stoned that he tried to order flowers with Interpol not
Interflora.
So he said.
          So I'm telling you.

But it's perfectly friggin plausible.
You know who we're dealing with.

*Before.*

The Foxtel Dawn Service,
led by the VB Governor-General.


*Before.*

Between grants and field work,
retail and clerical spots,
I had a neat line I didn't
much like in funny scripts.

I didn't partake, not
                    often.
Actually,
            can we define often?


*Before.*

She was there, at the funeral.
Will came because he'd loved my dad.
He still wanted to, with us,

but it was done with, even if
he was still, somehow, after
the runners, the stealing,

the cheating, the ridiculous drugs,
Will-fucken-Ridley, still a kind
of family.
            Tiny sandwiches, some

foul-looking dips, crackers, chips.
That window with the flaw in it
I swore was a ghost as a kid,

when I couldn't tell the difference
between a nail and a snail.
The last album I tried playing him,

refusing his age, or mine –
the *Hail to the Thief* remaster.
Drinking cheap red from his glass.

Across the room, Kate Willis. How
had I never noticed those eyes before.
How am I noticing them now?

In the hall outside dad's room, Kate.
Moving through from the kitchen
with a tray of what, it's Kate. Her fingers

glance across mine, handing me some
object. A plate. I won't take a pill, I
am going to be present. The back door

tsks behind me and stutters again
and I'm on the track down to the creek.
The bush wells and blurs, the fat wet heat

just is and the bank has fallen in just
a bit more again. I find another spot. Everything
spills out until there's nothing. And

here is Kate. And now she's holding me, rocking me,
smell of sweet sweat, her small mouth moving toward me.

                                        Oh, Daddy.


*Before.*

Days before Nan died
in the ward at Kurri
she asked, a bit feverish,

a bit off on the morphine,
*I heard Marg*
*say something about Pete.*

*Is he here? Where's your brother?*
I didn't know, so I told her
what he'd told me

before he said had to go.

*Before.*

The IVF was just fucked for Kate
and then the baby died.
His marbled skin, his silent tiny
kiss of a mouth. Weightless,

               almost,

he seemed.
          We gave him a name
we couldn't bear to tell anyone.

*Before.*

Ridley went to Sydney with my sister.
*With*, in every sense you can name.
The house, mum called it, staticky

with fleas. The time after, only vials
crunching like biscuits, like
eggs underfoot.

*No-one there, not a thing*
*of theirs left in the room.* So
Mum said.

*You know she's pregnant again?*
                  *What*

*do you mean, again?*

*After. The end of the impair.*

Out of the shelter before dawn
we go, into the dark wet noise,
the early lightning,
                    watchful.

We knew we were close to the edge,
*Nar, I'm sure it's fine.* He insisted.

Back at Vincent Street before dark,
if we can.
                At the bend, just still

dark, he opens his mouth
to the storm
but there's nothing to hear.

Another sound, sharp, I think,
and he's down in the river,
and I duck and weave

in the rain the path
down to the straggling
stumbling river to pull

him out from the wet,
the heavy, heavy wet, that
hard stinging fucking

pelting rain – fuck you –
rain in my heavy slow
clothes grabbing at him

any part with slipping
fingers to pull him just
reel him in – what a fish

you are – and lightning
scans him silver his skin

his scaly clothes and
onto the mud against
what

      an old wall, rocks,
dunno, wedge him
for the next move

the big manouevre and
looking out for a flash
from a muzzle or the

soft whip sound that hot
sharp punch waiting
for it it's trained on me

and I strain out of
the water the current
heavy but hardly moves

and I slide up and out
pinion I think yeah
pinion on out and a hand

stiff sore fingers curled up
wrist weakening bent wrong
in and around his sleeve

left sleeve almost balanced
well now and he's not
moved not one bit,

where is the shooter,
he hasn't moved not
on his own yet and slide him

up and out into the air
breathe come on thumping
his chest kissing breath

into him never thought
I'd pash you, mate, did
you, not working get

into that bit of scrub
look for the hole the
wound and there the huge

blunt welt on the side
of his head not an entry
or exit he's slipped,

you've slipped, haven't you,
and your head's hit those rocks,
so back up, it's a mess, you're a mess

aren't you, your poor stupid
careless head, shit it's
soft there isn't it, you poor

bugger let's get your
pack off and get you
under somewhere there's

no-one shooting well
not here not now
What? Am I speaking now?

Talking to myself,
so doesn't count.
Get us out of here, not

safe not good no
good breathe just
breathe cover him

up get back in and
bring someone with
to fix him up

when we can.

*Before.*

You know,
if Cessnock seceded,
the national dish
would be chips.

This isn't
a criticism.


*Before. Escalation.*

It's not as if it escalated quickly.
My mother would have said, *I seen better-run ruddy*
*housie nights.* Then the arrests. Then
the shootings, the one at Yarralumla.

Then the scene at Tullamarine, then
the AFP barracks and then someone or other
collapsed on the live cross
to the Committee's address to both Houses

about what had to be done and the when. Something
in the aircon, maybe, had sickened them, the ones who didn't
know what was up, those who hadn't
been told, and stayed until the division to vote.

*After.*

Plus,
he was a hard nut
who, Cal noted,
had *softened some
what.* But they'd kept
alive two years
or more, all of them,
and had let me in.
By let me in, I mean
caught me and made
use of me, when I thought
I was drifting carefully
after Neath went down –
Comancheros. *Go sentry
when you're asked, do
the rosters and kill
any cunt we tell you to.
You'll be right.* I did,
and I was. What else
was there I could do?
Thanks, Finn,
I suppose.

*After. Amnesty week.*

The stormwater drain you cross
on your way into Newcastle
is still signed *Styx Creek.*

*After.*

For a few days the churches were gluts
of armed parishioners and any number
of dead petitioners.

*Ruth. Before.*

*For the birds,*
                    she says, and turfs a scrap of pear
to ground. The rock doves – pigeons – coo
and are soft and brutal shovers to get at it.
Ants soon carpet the bits.
                              Across the park,
Council is pulling up a sheet of footpath
and grass below one of the ironbarks,
where native bees've laved and spat a hive (outside
her window's a wasp nest, a papier mache
disco ball).
                    You see the rise of roots, thigh- and wrist-
thick, pushing at the surface. The bees live a couple
of weeks, about as long as the ants, their cousins, who're
all over the fruit, and who ferry speck-sized bits
under the ground, into the dirt alongside coal,
fossil forests, slabs of Permian sunlight harnessed
and frittered on warmth across the grid instead of
slipping on a pair of tracky dacks, pulling out
the winter doona.
Tap or scratch at the nest for a cranky model
of how an atom works, or's supposed to look, if you
could look, radioactive with venom as the isotopes

buzz out, tangential, fizzing pain:
                              the same way, maybe,
the Coalfields' mines looked, after a cave-in, a fire, or
a shit boss who'd sparked off a strike with cheap gear
or no mind (read: *pocket*) for safety.


*After. Water cycle.*


Of course, it wasn't long
before those vast calved glaciers
fell on us as subtropical rain.


*Barely after. The next days.*


Neighbourhoods, whole suburbs
were tagged by someone logged in
as an admin
            as safe.
                    They weren't.
Hooded men with guns, clubs, blades,
grenades waited,
                hiding, strategic.
Or nail bombs,
              pipe bombs packed
with cutlery, glass, infected biopsy
samples, according to trolls that seemed
in the know enough, or too much.
I crept out through Hamilton on my way

a lucky week later, the backstreets
still shouty with barricades and empty checkpoints.
Down Beaumont, spooked by the clean silence there,
the fractured, shady reflections,
the eviscerated shop doors.
                              The relief
at getting through and into the sweating
shining wetlands – like taking a vast
and difficult shit.

This was when the power was still on
here and there, well, intermittently.


*Before.*


But that was when I still knew how to speak.


*First day after.*


The school's mufti day.
Gold coin donation.
But looks like a Ken Done jumper.
Just laying there.

*After. The waiting is the hardest part.*

They aren't here.
We send Hamid and Clydie up the line,
to see if they haven't overshot the meet.
But they wouldn't've, not Cat and Ember.
Those two are sharp AF.
                                    So we sit
and wait in the shade at the cemetery,
just above the kink in the road,
where the level crossing is.
                                    It's not like
we're desperate for the trade, but the soap
they promised 'd be nice.
                                    Rain the other side
of the hills south, around Freemans.
The rails glisten. Nothing.
A movement at the bend
is a pair of goats.
                                    Ember, where are you?
Amber. Honey, please make it.

*Before. Hacked.*

The Blue Cross's twitter account
claimed responsibility
for several glitter dumps
in Melbourne overnight.

*After.*

At the cocktail
party, as the light
outside paled a bit,

a kid's top
was set spinning
among the listless

frowning booze,
unsteady on its one
revolving point,

a misshapen planet –
the sharp crashing
sound of its slight

collisions, of the chat
and bickering, mostly
good-natured, but edging

to hard and uncivil when
the latest thing was placed
on the table or

stabbed on at the end
of a polished silver fork.
That day, and this and

every day orbits its
own brevity,
the light and sound,

the spectacle of
flares, fires, the noise
of feuding that burns

along the valley's hard
long fractures, pulling
in the slowly-spinning

ghosts, pressing in,
like those in the offshore camps
wanted in,

to intern and inter,
spooks from a past
we'd forgotten how

to remember, dumb
fucks we were, but
closed out by the bollards,

the fences, the sick-
staked ditches, the
tearing need to get

to someone, to get back
to her, but where, in time,
where in the ripping-away

of that time, of
memory and voice,
of the hollowed-out

families, as prehistoric
stars wander and circle
in the cold and towering

sky, in the dark
or the day, whether
we notice them

or not — the centrifuge
our lives are in now,
spinning out completely

beyond, fizzing as all
the bright and
sudden colour goes,

and
so do we.


*After. Parking station.*

All those cars
caked on top of each other, level
after level,
            still gleaming bright
under the automated glow of renewables.

*After.*

Photos of it, I saw in books as a kid,
on archived webpages – the river,
iridescent. Pollution's less visible now,

seeing we've stopped generating rubbish,
unless bodies count as rubbish, unless

the discarded, flood-snatched tidy towns are rubbish.
But then the pumps and levees and
machinery complained and sooner

or later stopped –
                    so the river
glows again now, day and night, its skin-thin
crust of chrome, shade of mercury, a viscous
ebb and drool into the ocean
from a slack-jawed mouth, which screams with gulls.

*Before.*

*Put them somewhere remote*
*and leave them there*
*or get rid of them,*
gargled their barometer
of charm, *whether the evidence*
*is there or not.*

Internment or interment,
he doesn't mind.
                    Careful now.

*After*

Which
empty future is it
am I aiming
to impress?
This thing that
looks like
a tangent but's really
a logical conclusion?
What happened
to the Reef?
The modest
exchange between India
and Pakistan?
Which MPs,
flapping up like
startled plovers,
made it
as far as New Zealand,
before the turnbacks,
the escort
out of sovereign airspace,
regardless of fuel levels;
on water matters,
manners.
   Her?
    Ruth.
     Kate.
What
  happened?

*After.*

The need to piss,
hours of stepping
methodically through
the few streets of
narrow old Neath,
is nearly too much —
the cramping, the stiffening
gait, but somehow
a relic of shyness
remains.
            He's
almost chivalrous
about it —
I drop and squat
between two stripped
cars in the twilight lane
and try to spill
my gush away from
my feet, feeling my
blush at the noise of it
rise like steam in the rapid cold,
and he turns his back,
as I watch his head
and know, for once,
he's still and watchful,
nearly tenderly so.
            So,
suddenly, carnal as hell
in the dirt, I ask him
to watch.
            *Please.*

*Before.*

The girl wearing her David Jones
houndstooth wrap as a cover
for her chemo hair loss
was taken as a Parramatta Intifada
insurgent and *quelled*, said the official mouthpiece.
No further comment follows.


*Not long before. October. Ruth.*

She must be thirteen by now.
You. You must.


*After.*

Sydney, that place is all ruin and rumour again.
But us, Newcastle, Maitland – we're settled: well,
choose a better word.

The new amnesty personnel swaps are working –
new blood in to stem the blood flow,
keep the lines open.

But I still miss someone.

*After. From beyond the Golden Highway.*

Past Dunedoo, they said, the roadblocks'd held.
That sounds like a euphemism, but anyway.
From there to Broken Hill, clean.
Army groups quarantined themselves until
the plague burnt itself out.
                              They're coming,
or they say they are. Or so somebody
says they are.
                    We'll wait. We'll see.


*Before. The commute.*

"Welcome to the Australia to Lithgow service."
Ha.


*Before. History Wars.*

Well, by their account, Hitler *settled* Poland
in 1939.


*After. Before.*

You have not been paying attention.

*After the storm.*

Rooves, or bits of them everywhere.
Not much to be done – out of the way
or re-purpose the crinkled sheets.

Up on the roof of so-and-so's old place.
She's long gone.
                A voice from down there,
saying, *Kel.*
                And a stranger, walking our way,
escorted with heavies. Friend of a friend.
                            *Got word.*
*He'd done a runner*
*last week.*
Ridley, he means.
Out before winter had time
to get in.
                *That Barrington mob,*
*pretty rough,* he said.
After telling me a woman
who sounds like Michaela is up there.
*But a kid? I don't know what*
*you're talkin about there. She didn't*
*have no kid with her, not up there, no.*

*Before.*

There were vigils near the end,
for the wrong people, so
then they came for the vigils.

*After.*

I wake up in the share room.
The air wet with snores
and someone quietly masturbating.

*Before. Craig, that's right.*

That one, I'd almost forgotten him.
I remember only the way he traced
his eyes over everything, constantly;

I remember what he tried on Michaela;
I remember his polycotton shirts,
his punitive cologne.

Mum could pick them, couldn't she.

*Before. National Archives.*

No need to burn the books
when you can let them rot.

*Before. For appearances.*

I dress as if I have no body.

*Before. After. Reciprocity.*

The river fronts were first
to go, floods of redcoats, we'd call them,
distributing blood and sick,

and gun-slung farmers,
horsemen and timber
getters, wives and shepherds

in sheds and houses
burning with slits —
and the people left mainly

died of plagues and trade, rape
and enough poison, starved on the fringes,
the least relics of their land.

All I got told until I found out
a bit was the place names
they might or mightn't've

dropped as they fell or fled,
only it was made to seem
somehow almost scenic —

Teralba, Boolaroo, Booragul,
Kurri Kurri, Murrurundi,
Wollombi, Cooranbong,

Quorrobolong,
Wangi Wangi, Bulga.
                              Gone,

they'd said – the Wonnarua,
Awabakal. The
Worimi, acknowledged

in the name of the children's court
at Broadmeadow.

What place do I have?
Who am I to remember?


*Before. Activities.*

Before we knew the scheme existed
(and only through Senate Estimates,
rumour and taps on the shoulder),
there was a system for informants.
                              And,
like so many policies these guys ran,
it ran like shit
                  down a toddler's
pants.
        Which meant neighbours
dobbing out neighbours, feuds
settled by vans pulling up at your
front door.
        I went way back
and so was 'required' –

I knew him, and was promised
in turn the best doctors. So I went to see him
again, felt dirty and hung out.

                        Did I believe
a word he'd said, or his crew?
                        Did I tell
either of my time-share handlers?
                                    I'd assumed
all appropriate staff were across the details.
Stupidly. Assume makes an ass out of u and me.
Shouldn't I have known?


*After.*

We're tunneling through the dark,
dad driving his freezing EK, and
to stave off sleep, to stay awake,

head against the rear door, the window,
I'm singing through
                        the names of the places
we skim through,

rattling them off in order, long knotted strings
of them, and skip ahead on the side roads
I know are coming up, scooping up
the miles of night as we go:

Bucketty, Laguna, Bulga, Broke,
Wollombi, Millfield,
Pelton, Paxton, Bellbird:
                        red cat's eyes
burst up from the black shoulders,
small skids of anxiety – what if

he falls asleep, what
if he misses the turn –


        or Cooranbong,
Freemans, Mulbring, Mount Vincent,
Kearsley, Abernethy –


        these long
and wordy maps, the little remembered places
in between, 've saved my life, tied
me over –
        that hidden gully off behind
the screen of scrub as you make that slight
curl into Kitchener, headed for Quorrobolong;


the track up to high ground
between those farmlets off
Wollombi Road; a small lip into the cave


that looks like a scar of blackberry and once
belonged to Yellow Billy, blackfella bushranger
who Ridley would swear was family.


Cessnock, Neath, Abermain, Sawyers,
Bishops Bridge, Keinbah.


Don't all places kind of line up,
in a tangle, their layout and backroad
connections making sense


to use when you need it:
        keeping ahead
of a fistful of blokes
you weren't expecting –

Denman, Sandy Hollow, Merriwa, Cassilis,
The Golden Highway –

keeping a couple of hundred yards
between you, shredding your lungs because
you know what's just ahead –

Sandy Creek Road, Sanctuary
Road, Cedar Creek Road, up into the hills
past Millfield –

if you can just get there
to that corner,
that quick bend,
                    you need to put a gap
on them, keep riding that pain in your thighs –
you know it'll fall
                    right
                         away,
the endorphins pulsing in

to save you and you know
they'll keep pitching around the long curve

and you're gone
sudden in a sprint across
and down under to the creek,

into the jammed dry culvert where you hope that
stash is still saved for just in case.
                              You do this and
feel them jolting, jogging above, and

remember then that small, quiet and
sure love for your dad, as if he's somehow
there, not exactly with you,

and feel a small blink
of smacked-out regret at everyone
who's died slow and long,
                                        and a vast
and weary relief you aren't with them
yet in the world's endless cemetery;

and you know you have to go soon
out the back of Kurri and tend
your father's weedy plot

                                out in the open,
killing sun.

It's a risk.
I'm glad
        I spent my life running,
and Dad always driving, away
from somewhere.

*After. After the long walk back.*

Walking home in the earliest morning
with Michaela, recovering, daughterless.

The blank dark air vibrating
and shunting in and through
the trees (near the old colliery,

aren't we?), making that low
and keening sound almost like

an ocean, collisions of water
and something harder than water –
crop of rocks, half-sunk rank

of ferry terminals, the new island
at the breakwater's end – caution

of rain: out of creekbeds, then,
and gullies, though they make for easy
travel until you're approaching the source.

I don't understand why I feel suddenly
tender towards her.

The fog's advice
is a muffling internet, a wellbeing
website that bells out its mediaeval

remedies, which is mainly what we have, anyway,
now. Though its baffling of sound

makes moving easier, less of a washing-over
of constant nerves and hard attentions.

The things people
will say. Wanting what used to be

a fancy, true, no proofs available
now against them.
                    Which was why


I wanted the library shored up,
at least half-guarded. You never

know, I said (*wrote!*) to Committee,
appealing to their practicality,
meaning,
                    You never know what you'll
need to know.
                    And they agreed —
*Good. We'll keep an extra eye on.*
                                    They're far
from stupid. I'm getting watched, too,
for speaking up, silent, like.
Drops from the down-pointing
leaves, any new smells rinsed

and surprising in the cold, which is
a tough thin blade against hands
and feet — the useful limbs.
                    *Get moving,*
*you lug,* Michaela says.
                    That's a new one.


Our noses are new animals, young
and worrying at novelty but needful,
curious.
                    Neither of us speaking —

our whole lives, our history, our long arrangement,
in the brittle frosty listening we need to do.
My gut gurgles with mistrust,
my lips purse tight and curl.

There was the time in the supermarket,
in the frozen goods' sharp and chiming cold,
us hoping for out of season fruit – dark plums,
the glistening syrupy light of them
making a sweet film on our bright chins,

and we'd fall into pits of laughing
at home, once we get there, eyes and gobs
agog, shining.
                    *What I've done, hon,*

*to get back to you?* she asks.

                              What do I say?
What do I want to say?

*What the fuck have you done*
*with Ruth.*
                    *Tell me or I will*
*definitely kill you.*

So I say it.

*Before.*

My year as a digilante
among the encrypto-fascists.

*After.*

The out-crew is back,
what's left of them.
A tactical withdrawal –
i.e. not getting
themselves all killed.
The plan for Maitland's
a total bust.
The guys with the head tatts.
*Jem's face turned to a zipper.*
Not ideal.
               So they give me
the job – *Well, you*
*know, you spent months*
*and months out there*
*on your own and hardly*
*a scratch*
               *to be seen.*
Committee know me
well, they say: quiet,
riskless, vengeant.
But please note:
               *to be seen.*

*After. Relief.*

The siren goes up
from a convoy up from the port.
We let them in, we didn't know,
not yet, the whole back story.

The dead belong
                    to all of us,
their blackening bones, their flags
of rotting polycotton.

                    The relief
came on sudden, heavy,
maybe like a siege.

*Before. Mum's dead.*

I refused to go to the funeral.
And I regret it, yes,
                    but I know
I'd regret going more.

*Before. Grandfather.*

He knots his fist again.
I wait out the damp slap.
It follows his wheezing breath
as he drops it to my back

my head my face my tits.
Then the leather slips its loop
and it begins. He did this
but it was my mother
put the idea of going
into my little head.


*After.*

That's the place, the house
we thought the witches lived —
back a bit from the street, hidden
off with oleanders, the grass

too long, no car, the yard
vibrating with cats, curtains
that shimmered and stuttered
as we skipped or rode past,

singing our get home safe rhymes.


*In the library. After.*

Emily Dickinson totally
was a hottie.

*Before.*

Baby fence skinks
on the back door mat

two days
after winter solstice

You understand
the farmers' concerns.


*Cactus. After.*

On Blackwood Street,
between
the storm-water drains,

across the road from
each other are two night
flowering cactus

in matching terra cotta pots,
throwing out their
velvet or something scent,

flirting with each other,
each broad white mouth
ogling the other, wanting

whatever small animal
they evolved with and which
doesn't live here to blend their pollen,

to suck at their nectar,
and, rubbing a long and tender
snout nosing in one

then the other.
Kate licking me out
against her back fence

at dawn. TMI, I know.
Your grandad's mum
had one, too —

I remember it, down
at Budgewoi, and then
in that grim home

at The Entrance, where
it was amateurishly pruned,
and all the rest of it.


*Before.*

After that first big rash of bombings,
and just before reports
of the virus spread
into suburb-by-suburb panic,

and while the TV was still on,
stories mushroomed about how
this would affect property prices.

The jury was out.

*After. The list.*

There was a list.

A small gang had it,
furnished like a prize,
weaponised.

       They went
camp to camp, later
town to town, looking
for its contents.

       When
they found Patriots, Blue Cross,
the usuals, they took their sweet time.
Axes to grind. You know the drill.


*After. Recriminations.*

Who wasn't relieved
or happy or felt avenged
(or needed avenging)

when the coup
came? Was it even a coup?
They still called it

Parliament, after all.
After all those months of it,
ratcheted up,

a narrative nearly perfectly
administered –
                Newspoll
with a body count.
                  But then
they started grabbing people
off the street, and not always
the ones you'd expect.

*After.*

Cholera.

*Before. It made no sense. I was six.*

Searching for xmas presents in the cupboard
and someone charges through the door.
Mum crying – groaning – on the whimpering bed.
Don't move, don't breathe.
                Through the crack
in the door –
grandad, wriggling around on top of her.
Mum's crying but she's smiling.,
her skirt all rucked up
using those bad words.

*After.*

She was Amber
until arson became our trick shot.

Then, *voila*! Ember!


*After.*

*Just lean on those fucks a little,*
he said,
            *they'll fold like*
*one of them tourist maps,*
he said.
            Leon.
Finn paid them a visit,
and I went with.


*Before. In.*

But this time he seems
nervous, twitchy, eyes
everywhere but on me.

Most of the other guys
aren't.
            Nervous.
The gates open,
in comes a new ute.

He says, switching,
*Hey, can you show Kel*
*the…*

It's not a request.

*Before. Missing the point.*

People were dopey enough to attack the fascists
on the grounds of their video production values.

*Before. Thinking.*

Hang on, did he just
piss me off? Those crates
in the ute's flatbed – clean,
dull metal, printed with something.
I got a look at the driver
but his passenger,
he didn't budge. Not while I was watching.
Do they know, or suspect? Or.
Or are they actually disciplined,
now? How'd these dumb fucks
get like that, so sloppy since forever,
like him. This new thing is like,
like, a new suit on him.
It's amazing, but doesn't fit.
Amazing, but not in a good way.

*Books.*

John Safran, *Depends what you mean by extremist.*
Densey Clyne, *Wildlife in the suburbs.*
*Dig Tree*, Sarah Murgatroyd.

Smell of mould in the library,
but as if somehow distant.


*After.*

READY?
READY?
READY?


*After. Shoes.*

Faded maroon dress sneaker
by Macbeth.


*Before. After court.*

Ruth driven away,
just as I walk out.
Oh, her eyes. Palm on the window.

*After. Acknowledgement of Country.*

*This is Wonnaruah country,*
                              *mate,*
we say to the stranger.
*Better come say hello.*

The man's smiling,
says, *I was wondering*
*whose place this was*

*all the way in.*
                *From where?*
Finn asks, gruffer
than usual. *Dubbo.*

*Where the government is.*
Well, that's new,
we hadn't heard this one before.


*Before.*


Armed guards on buses, trains
and at stations
seemed a great idea to some,
those who could be convinced
that there was something to lose,
but the first guy they shot
was just avoiding a fare,
and so was the second.

*Before. State.*

In the State, Ridley said,
there'd have to be something,
or some clue about Yellow Billy.

I never quite got why
he thought what he thought.
He never made it clear.

And so when nothing turned up, no
letters, no reports, no documents that said
anything much at all,

he gave up. When he stopped giving up
he started calling adoption agencies –
he couldn't be theirs,

could he? Not really, he was sure.


*After. Honey.*

Honey,
this lump
is getting bigger,
and me weaker. I
might
        never find you.

Your mum's here, now, but,
well, you *know*.
She doesn't know
what I've done.
She could probably guess.

There's this gum,
a big scribbly that shines
almost silver in the late
arvo. Behind the old
shops, on that rise.

I love it
            there, here; it's where
I'm writing from now.


*After. Used to be an orchard.*

Sunset. Night races in
toward this thin roadside —

the mandarin trees just
ripening now,

each fruit a small dull sun
with the sun on it.

*Before.*

I've got a bad feeling about this.


*Trigger. Just before.*

I knew before the handlers.
I didn't tell them.
                    It wasn't

Ridley they were watching at all,
Ruth stashed somewhere,
but that little weed – never got his name:

'him', 'he' all I ever caught –
always at his ear, hunting a sneer
around a room, tracking it.

The way he talked about Ruth.
My pen in my pocket. Uniball

fine point. Blue. He knows
I'm here and thinks he's watchful.
He has no clue,

that night, as the biro's point
pushes in through his carotid,
arms pinned now and he's

choking out on the floor. Good.
What he said he would do with her.
Said he had.

But I thought it was just
bombs they had. Containable.
I was going to tell in the morning.

He'll never fucking
                    touch her
again.

The next day, in retaliation,
I suppose, thinking they were busted,
they undid the canisters.

Stupid.
        Why don't you think.



*After.*


Scurvy.



*My little bolthole. After.*


My little bolthole – a pit
barely the size of me
nuzzled under an iron sheet,

wasted with rust, and itself
lodged into a dense-looking
thicket of wattle that actually

gives easy, noiselessly.
Just down from here and the gullies
like it tapered in among these ridges,

weatherboard houses
from I don't know when, maybe
the 40s, yellow, powder blue, pink.

I know their loungerooms,
the flu-dead and plague-dead
slumped on sudden recliners

or in bed, I know their names,
decades back, the patterns
the damp makes climbing

into the mould,
                          I know too well
the layout of their bedrooms,

and I know the tics and
plaints and habits of their tight
slack-piped bathrooms and outdoor loos,

the trails you'd see of small pads
that made their way across the
*bastard of a late frost overnight*

*that did the fucken*
*strawbries in,*
> unless, that is,

you felt it was too far to go out
in that heavy dark and piss
instead crouched under

the rough lemon tree.
> You don't really

need me to tell you how I know all this,
do you? I'm being a bit cute again,

> aren't I?

This is what I think of, waiting
for whoever it is to piss off.
> He seems

to think he's being patient.
> He's near,

but I'm listening for the wrens
that weave through the undergrowth
to start their tiny piping again. Plus,

through the smallest slit
in the corrugations I see his shadow
hover and waver.
I've got all day. All week.

*Before. Public telephone.*

A woman resembling my sister
speaks Methadone
into the black plastic cup.
Oh.


*Before.*

No-one sure how that rail car
past Ellalong got there,
or when.
       For a while, Ridley
hung out there, after his mum.
I mean *weeks*. And by hung out,
he lived there, half-camping.
One night he came
tapping my bedroom window –
*Kel, I seen something. I*
*think*. Swore on it.
         He waited
and watched after the first one,
at the game trails from the car
all night – cats, the odd rabbit,
owl-freaked, adjusting his eyes
to the permanent dark, his
ears to the quiet snuffling
birds make, or something does,
and a week after the first one,
a black thing, squat, *fucken noisy*

*as, spot of white at its arse.*
                              Then
another one, arguing.
                    *Babe,*
*they're* not *supposed to be here.*

What's not?
                    *Devils,* he said.
At first I thought he mean the red guys,
with horns.


*After. A week of watching Finn.*

Always picking at
or touching his face –
stray eyelashes, what feels
like a scratch or sore? –
wiping it as if to clean it
with his spread hands
covering, for a moment,
his eyes.


*After. The arrangement.*

Word is in Newcastle
they got the lights
back on – the whole

grid, but patchy. Not up here,
but someone might get sent.
They cherry-pick us,

won't admit just anyone
who wants in. That
sounds familiar. Though

they farm out drugs
and doctors, and don't,
generally, shoot at us

anymore. We're dotted out
along their edges – listening
posts, outliers paying a loose tribute

with our blood, our eyes,
what we can cadge
from the country.

We know – we hear –
they're talking to what's left
of Sydney. And rumours –

people coming down from the north –
and vague things you could never
be sure of: China's landed ships,

or Indonesia, or boats full
of people escaping nuked Iran.
I don't know that that actually happened.

People talk shit.
I want to see the lights
one night with you, Ruth,

and then come back.


*Before. Anniversary dirty weekend.*

Kate's made the booking – a surprise.
Half-drunk from the sunny bar,
I float over to reception with her,
my Long Island Iced Tea sweaty
between my fingers.
                        *Name?*
asks the officious thing at the counter.
My mouth sprays a bright fountain
of booze across the in-set uplights
when K comes back with Mr and Mrs
Clitheroe.
                  With a hard 't'.
We were so young then. Weren't we?


*After.*

*No, I was only clearing*
*my throat.*
                  Not *giving*
*my opinion.*

That's
what that look means.

Though I don't say that.
I don't say anything.
Not ever.


*Before. Schoolbags.*

Shaun lived across the road,
across the train line
from the little colliery under the hill –
he lived in a shack of a place
we called the Gilberts.
I tell mum I want a schoolbag
like the one Shaun has. Her eyes
go back, white in her head,
and it's another thing
I add to my list of what I don't
understand but know I can't
ask Miss Cussons at school
even though she's what I now
know was solicitous.


*After. Archery.*

Early in the mist
at the edge of the scrub
at the old archery range

hoping on roos.
The straw colour just now
coming into the grass.

We wait, get slowly
downwind. One of them crouches
to the ground and nibbles.


*Before.*

Janelle and Mrs C dropped me
home after – the three of us see
Mum splayed in the stairwell
of the flats making out
with the milko, his hand
right up her nighty, the yellow
floral one, not even
a nice one.


*Before.*

Ridley wakes and tells me his dream.
A small girl, giggling. A daughter,
his daughter, he guesses.
                    *Don't*
*you dare put one of those in me,*
I'm only half-joking.
                    I can barely
imagine getting it out, and I
wince, involuntary.

*Before. Complicity.*

And I'm in the alley
lodged between the skip
and the wall, still shaking and
out of breath. Pubs along here
hawk out brawlers, the odd
someone shouting
almost intelligibly up the street.
One guy in blue says
to his partner, *Officially*
*worst shift ever. Just dead*, as if full stops
glotted the gaps there, his shoulder
suddenly squawking as the windows
along the strip blow in,
the quick white wiping him
and the street into silence.

*Before. What she told me.*

Dad home later
than usual from the TAB.
Called her outside.
(I vaguely remember
this.) The car was a mess,
the passenger side all
crumpled metal, the paint
lifted and cracked like the mud
in the bottom dam. And then
she screamed, enough
that the neighbours rang,

*Was she alright?*
                    She was
jealous, is what she was –
she'd wanted it to be her,
to smash the car and herself,
to drive off in a fit and
finish it, what she'd wanted
for years, to make whatever
it was she felt or
didn't feel stop.
                    She hoped
that would make it stop.

Or this is what I'm guessing.
She'd never say.


*Before. Carpet burns.*

Carpet burns on my knees
and forearms, my lower back.
Ridley's are everywhere,
rashes of half-torn skin,
emblem of where we rooted
til long after it hurt.


*Before.*

Drinking with Kate and thingo,
I lost count at four – I was

completely mortal,

                    such a little

thing.


*Before.*

Up hard, close.
I smell the danger on her
and taste it, her hard
and dirty probing
rises in me, the birdsong
in her throat (her
throat) wants me, and
there, grit or something
on her neck, from
earlier, on the ground,
and behind her damp
hair. I'm breathing
in hot chokes.
The danger if Kate knows,
ever.
     Then
in comes her husband,
gripping something.


*Before. Epistles.*

The difference between love
and lose
is one letter:

Dear Kel, something your sister,
something baby, something Ridley.

*After.*

I try to learn a place by watching
what birds do above it.

*Before. Before him.*

I didn't have anyone.
Dad,
        I guess.
See what I mean?

*After. Not exactly birdsong.*

Trying to not get killed
when, harder to trace
than a whipbird call,
a quick squawk and squeal
of a radio, with a gunshot.

I drop and my guts do too.
A scratching sound. Feet
on leaf litter, sticks.

A lyrebird close, nosing for food.
Fuck.
    Me.
        Dead.


*After.*

Beats going on a witness protection program I suppose.


*After. Before.*

The pane is dusty
(and so is the pain [nyuk
nyuk nyuk]).

        When the sun
falls on it early in the morning
just as it spills over and across

the horizon, it looks like
a relief map spotted with soaks,

billabongs, ephemeral streams,
spatters of salt lakes or depressions,
or the deep scatter across the sky

of stars, smeared and indistinct
through tears, smudged glass,
sun- and virus-wrecked eyes.

Stuff burns up in the sky —
satellites re-entering,
their long orbit wobbling in decay,

then a bright magnesium flare —
once I swear there was a hiss,
a slight sharp little sound,

a distant piss.
                    A rain comes
and changes the course of these

grainy rivulets, clarifying
the view, wiping the map into
a seeming blank until the drying heat

rises again and the old patterns
emerge, subtly changed,
features climbing out that hadn't

been there before. Wattle blossoms
slurp up the rain and here, small tendrils
cling to the screen, ribbon of the sun

we spin around effortlessly,
all those cycles going around — dark,
moon, blood, spring, the summer virus

resuscitating and as it pulls pieces of light
through itself, refracting and sparking off shards
of rainbow as if from the spilt oil

coiling into the still-damp mud
beside that truck, the tanker, left there
by the back road past Mulbring

toward Quorrobolong, something awful,
something typical must've happened
to the driver – I imagined, then,

when I still could. No marks, no nothing,
just an empty cab, the busted tap at the rear
drooling the thick black spit

which was, anyway, quickly running low
everywhere as we stand around
looking down on out vertiginous future.

And then
            just forgetting it could matter.

This window. It's a good window.


*Nostalgia. After.*

You know, forget nostalgia:
the burning future pings on out ahead
without us, like a non-returning sonar.


*After.*

Dysentery.

*Before. Car bombs.*

The spooks didn't always share
with the cops. I worried then that Ridley's mates
in that crew might've taken my car for a bomb.
I didn't, stupid, report it. Wasn't it enough
I helped them into other cars, locked carparks,
playing the cute little decoy on the side?


*Before.*

Left in the backseat
with a pile of books
on backstreets – Wollombi Road,

Scout Halls, family dos,
quick drop-offs for Michaela
that turned into long cuppas

and a smoke out the front.
*Asterix, Choose Your Own Adventure.*
*My Book of Volcanoes.* Dad's

hand-me-downs, things
he never let go of. Once
I tried the cigarette lighter

in the old VC Commodore.
But only the once.
I'd need a toilet where or when

there wasn't one. I'd wait,
and I'd waited, reading,
watching, listening. Stretched

hours of it.
                    Once this man kept
walking past, doing laps

around the block, an eye half
on me, half on who else was around,
and, on maybe the seventh time,

tapped on the window,
eyes shifting left, right, but not
watching his own back –

where dad suddenly was, clearest focus
I've ever seen on anyone.


*Before.*

Dad's tic in his left eye,
which he doesn't ever
acknowledge. Kate would've
just squirmed, if we'd been together

when he was alive: but Ridley,
young Will Ridley never did.
Proactive,
                is our Will. Dad asking
the next day, after finally getting

to meet him, frowning, *What*
*the hell was up with loverboy*
*last night?*
      Shit, I think, he
heard us? Gross. Gawd,
and I'm actually blushing. *What*
*do you mean?* You can imagine
the tremor as I speak. I bet
I'm blushing all over.
              *You know,*
*what was that little spazz doing last night,*
*winking at me*
          *the whole time?*


*Before.*


In the car, waiting for him, engine
ticking over in the hot wind, a block away
from where he says he's staying and the front
yards along here, all across this flat town,
aren't lawns anymore, they look like

that bleached buzzcut that'd once been
the new thing for a few months years ago
and so I cut the motor after more than
twenty, thinking *another three minutes,*

or *just another five*, seeing shadows
lengthen from around the weatherboard corner –
here he is now; but no. I wait and keep on waiting.

I chill as sweat dries in warm dry waves. Cunt's not
coming, is he, I think, and I know that I'm set, and just go anyway.


*After. Where is she, Michaela?*

*He took Ruthie, not too long*
*after it started, you know, a while,*
*maybe six months, when some*
*scary guys came after him.*

                    *We heard*
*they was coming, yeah, and so*
*they went, talked, well, went on*
*and on, more like, about*
*getting out past Merriwa, around there,*
*away from where they knew who*
*he was, knowing what he done,*
*and he wanted to see what*
*happened the other side*
*of the range, the divide. Yes,*
*the Golden friggin Highway.*
*Still that. I know.*
*I know.*
            *Never gave up on it.*
*He thought something must've*
*been doing round Dubbo, somewhere*
*out there, thought different groups,*
*the density, might stop the bug*
*spreading so far, or as fast as it done*
*in the cities. Unless, that is,*
*everyone'd tried crossing, maybe*
*over the Great Western. Hey,*

*Great Western, wasn't that*
*your favourite bubbly?*
Does she ever breathe?

*And you, you just let them go, just*
*let him take her?*, I say.

Really, honey, by then
I've just switched off.
Again.
            Sorry. I'm sorry.


*Before. Water table.*

It wasn't mine owners' kids
who lived in the catchment areas
where the longwall cracks
dropped the levels just as temps
began to plateau high
with real consistency.


*Before. Ruth.*

You could've been mine.

Let me draw you a picture:
me at fifteen, part Wednesday
Addams, part Tuesday's child.

Is that you, too?

*After.*

That stash of Coke we lucked on,
cartons upon cartons of it,
we sealed and buried near the river
as winter hit as relief for once summer
churned around again. Holy shit:
that first rush of sugar in my gut,
my teeth – the first in years,
my poor sour head reeling with
it like a harsh spike of shockingly bad speed.


*Before? After?*

An hour ago my feet were wet,
watching the broad shallow tide
slide and piss away – the inlet
draining itself. Back

I came, to pretend at looking after
my alleged mum; back here where
there's no nurture in the family or

in the land, in the deep still creeks
slurped at by feral willows, the long
wide slots of forest gone to powerlines,
of the freeway paralleling old rail

the mines don't use anymore –
they've been bust 50, 60 years,
though *This is still mining country,*

a bloke at the bus stop or a laminated
history at the library'll say.
The freeway runs past here
to Singleton to feed and fuel the commute;

back here to the old shops guised-up
as new shops, fronts for start-ups, pop-up
studios; back to where meat ant nests

like boils, or acne scars,
pock the dry hard soil, *the dirt, we call it here* –
its thin and crusty shale out above
the gullied-in farmlets:

here where provocation is sitting in a pub,
waiting nose-in-a-book, or glancing around: what
to drink in next. The self-talk

when I come back's meticulous,
malicious, but still I come, long
after her any other family's gone.
Her catastrophising guilt she won't ever

speak of, not to me –
difficult and slippery to step around
as leeches in sandals on a Sunday School picnic.

But I come back,
don't I,
            knowing from the out
what's coming.

More than fifteen years away,
shady side of thirty, Kate
on my arm, in my bed, guessing

what we'll get made out to be
by her housie snobs, her shitty random roots
and neighbours,
the tradies I'll have to book in

if I ever
want any kind
of inheritance,

you know, even assuming.
Red shreds of cloth
all through the bush here, tied to banksia,
to turpentines, tying off

where the path is.
                    Still,
we only lasted six weeks

up in the mountains –
washed back up to the valley,
near enough to escape
to the sea.

*After. The sun.*

The sun, late in the afternoon,
on the thin blond grass
dangling up in this stretch
of open woodland.
                          I'd want
to lie down in it, soaking deep
warmth in, head on a shoulder,
or someone's on mine, reading, or,
like that other time I was with you,
the nearly-year you lived with us,
and it looked like, maybe it might last.
That rustling we worried was a snake
in the leaf litter and grass
was that echidna, snuffling out a long

string of ants at our picnic,
right up to your toes with its snout,
your giggle something pure,
Kate and us making up shapes out
of the shifting clouds.
                          *They look*
*like mummy's plates. No, that one's*
*just a cloud,* you say, as if
it were some new thing you were
trying out, not sure how it worked.

                          Anyway.
That's it.
          That's all I wish for.

*Spooks. Before.*

They knew quite a bit about me,
been asking questions,
I suppose, but who of?

Wanted me in, made promises –
no threats, nothing like that.
*Just a quick drop in, say hello,*

they knew exactly where he was.
*You get to see the niece,*
she says, *We can talk about custody,*

*again, after we're done.* As if it were an add-on,
not the whole deal.
It was politically difficult

because his – their –
platform was similar to that
pig of a senator, though

they saw no direct evidence of a link.
They suspected the car bombs
and wanted to know more.

Only the car bombs,
                    they thought,
but worried enough.

And which side were they working, anyway?
That's what I think about now,
one of the things.

*Before. Finn fin. God.*

An infection
from a cut
in his foot.

His last words,
grinned out, quoting
until the end. Typical.

*You're my only friend,*
*and you don't even like me.*

Of course I lost it,
at last, bawling out loud.


*After. Traveling light.*

No new shoes to be had:
but choose anyway the road's hard shoulder
over the half-melted tar —

jolts my shoulder
up through the spine.
Stiff in anticipation.

The small kit on my back
is a sweat trap. Dried food
in packets a year past the use-by,

plastic poncho, bottles (three
water, one salvaged Jamesons),
painkillers, antibiotics, a bunch

of twine, changes of clothes.
Lightweight portable cookers
Topo maps, a fistful, in order.

Ammo. Shoe polish for moving
at night in case of. Knives on me
already, 9 mil auto my arse pocket.

Doped up on codeine until. Sloppy.
Onto the plateau from the west,
work out their disposition

from there.
                    Disposition?
Let's get past Maitland first.


*Before.*

I'm clearing the leaves, raking my back
out of place when I notice my shadow is gone:
the wind angles around and the smell

in the quickening dark is light but hard.
Leaves flame into ash, warm and murderous
whispers on my bare shoulders, my glowing face.

Into that burning fury I flicker,
moving like I never had, wanting to save
the house, our house, almost forgetting

to get myself somewhere properly safe.
Can I make it to the creek? The grass there
already a thin blaze, and vanishing

in the warping air. The wet backyard's all steam.
The dangling fire, the sheets of flash, the silence
inside the noise. How am I in the car.

High beams strike along the footpath. *Don't
do that.* We go back the day after,
the jacaranda we planted behind the fibro

's just a small black rake, the fence out the back
all tripwires and stubs. The fireys just say
*The wind,*
            *it just*
                    *changed.*
They'd as good as given it up.

Entirely contrary
to forecast. So we rang up
a painter to lay on a new coat

and rinsed the smoke out,
grinning through the tears.
*Geeze, hand me a fucken dart,*

laying on the local idiom.
That's my Kate,
                    a quick study.



*Before. Holidays and the drought that wasn't.*

Hard to believe now
people were taking their dinky
little holidays even as it must've been clear
everything was wrong.
                    We did,
too, ignoring, or complicit,

driving south through the glary
whitened grass dripping along
the steep verges that funneled the harsh
invisible light down the freeway
curling metallic over and round the steepening hills.

Ruth, from the back of the car,
*I need a tissue, Aunty Kel.*
                    *Really?*
*What for sweetie?*

*I need a tissue for the lip balm*
*that came out of the unicorn's bottom.*

*After. Learning proportion from Finn.*

So I brought a gun
to a fist fight.
AK. Customised.
Silencer, flash
suppressor. Extra
mags on my belt.
Stripped right
down. Well, I like
to be prepared. Those
others, they looked
at me as if I'd shat
in the lift.
             *Seriously?*
*Dude.*
      But backing
right the fuck off
just the same.
          Back
in town, he had the
living shit
beaten out of me.
I make each mistake
just the once.

*Before. Kate the nurse.*

I never was one for uniforms, before,
but, shit, she looks fine
in those pale blue scrubs,
home late, her eyes glazing over –
a film of weariness and lust.


*Before. The drugs.*

I tripped down off my teetering high
and smacked my mouth
on the glinting floor of Coles,
poster girl for you name it –
hard work, small dreams, crank,
oxies: what else have you got?


*After. Posters.*

take land    grow food
learn to fight    tear down fences
learn medicine    destroy what destroys you
organise, without leaders and bosses
take care of your neighbours    make police obsolete
sabotage instruments of control and surveillance
steal, make and share everything you can

Kept the flyer from that.

*Before. Exile.*

I can't fucken wait to not go back.


*After. Hard.*

The first months were brutal.
The things I saw – I can't even.
An old youtube clip someone posted, years before,
thinking it hilarious, which in truth
it was, is what I kept thinking of –
a pelican at a waterside park scoops up

in its bill one of a dozen pigeons scratching
at the ground. It keeps flapping in there, one
wing flopping out at the side, and nearly
escaping, nearly getting out, until it doesn't.


*After. Verbatim.*

*I looted the pub, the chemist*
*and the cake shop, he said.*
(It was hardly a boast, more

an itinerary.)
                    *There wasn't*
*the shooting and the bombs*
*up here. The shooting come*

*later but. Oh, and I did the real*
*estate agents, too, I reckon*
*they were Jews. That's where all*

*the paper's from, the real estate.*
*I wanted something to draw on.*
*You're using it too, aren't you?*

*And so then I just locked the doors,*
*smashed the windas and torched the cunt.*
*It really went up. Noisy too . . .*
                                        *Yeah,*

*I did. Leave them. Inside that is.*
*And not long after that – people*
*was already tooling up the freeway but*

*some stopped here for a bit. Bit*
*of a mess at the roundabout but most things*
*were still running. But then, that's when lots*

*started getting sick and they died*
*real quick. Coughing, the spots – they*
*turned into those gross lumps after*

*maybe three days and then dead. Loads*
*of them dead, and then* we *started croaking*
*too. Hardly any cars, well, few dozen,*

*come up from Sydney the back way.*
*Must've forgotten Wollombi Road.*
*Unless it got cut off – maybe somethin*

*bad went down down there. Nobody said.*
*So who knows. They started kicking it*
*so we found out who of them*

*was going to be useful, figured this was*
*going to last a while. Shot the rest.*
*Could of all been sick. If we'd knew,*

*would of saved the ammo. Took a long*
*time for anything to go on the improve.*
*Yeh, good to have the dam goin again.*

*Cops couldn't do much about the fightin*
*or they didn't wanna. Until they got*
*the army in to lock us down.*

*From Singleton, yeah. It was once the guns*
*started comin out. Still, we had that little*
*window, a few hours, to get a few things done.*

*Not that I had any scores or nothin*
*to settle, but I could of. The cunt who did*
*go nuts though, you wouldn't of picked it,*

*it was one of the solicitors.*
*Name of Keiths. Keith and Keith. Used to be*
*quiet as. Didn't last long.*

*We couldn't of let him.*

*After. Your mum.*

Your mum acts like she knows something.
What do you think?


*After.*

Sprayed on the sign at Neath,
Cessnock bRoadS.
That us.


*After. The blouse that I liked.*

Here in the half-shade,
the mellow light lanced
by the red-green of dangling gum tips,

a light burr of cicadas
off somewhere distant enough

to level it down to amp hiss
(that band we had in our teens –
The Pants – all reverb, fuzz

and three chords),
the birds not clichéd – eastern

spinebills, a whipbird, wattlebirds
phlegmy in the sweet nectar smell
behind where I don't need anymore

to look, a Torresian crow, their range
soaking further south season by season,

some kind of small parrot way above
where I'm sitting – and the road,
of course it's quiet now that we've

stilled it, but the stink, which I always
loved, of melted tar rises and drifts

as the sun pours across it for hours, weeks;
my skin tickles as if there were slow
ants across me, as one day they will;

the damp steady drone of small
native bees; shafts of light hitting

the dirt, the ground litter, lizards
all askitter to drink at it; the slower
swaying of a brown snake, cautious

but strangely cocksure. For this long trip
to you, I kept that light blouse

I liked (blouse? a blouse it is)
I found in that left-open house
a year or so back. I'm not sure

I can get back up right now.
Is that a breeze

coming up now?
                    Good.
Good.


*Before. Hotel meet with the spooks.*

I'm sure these two were carrying,
but working hard to look as if
they weren't. The lift was slow,
it seemed it was barely moving
at all.
            I wanted to give it a kick
to be sure. The doors open,
gliding,
            after not long at all,
to the glare and fuzz
above the harbour and rooves. His voice
familiar, the white sky behind him
blots out all but his outline, the soft
close frizz of hair. *So,*
                        he says,
waiting for what, I honestly don't know.

*Before. Walking across the park, not looking at the family picnics.*

Sun's cooling now through the upper branches.
Ironbarks. The line they make, a dawdling curve,
really, follows the creek's concreted banks.
One black bird plunges, another in its wake, shadowing it.

Torresian crows – should they even be here? – smaller
than ravens. In the bench shade the one grapples
a cheese stick, gives its eyes a few angles at it, appraising
a new thing, which it is, and peels it open – defter,

more sure than the six year old who'd abandoned it,
the uncles not looking like help – and bills the strings
of cheese out, head rearing back with the tugged and yellowed

intestines. Busy slurping, so the other ducks in, pulls
the rest free, dirts it up, strops it against the timber seats
in a dark temper.
                    Crows for you, bless 'em.

We were here with you, six months ago.


*Before. Safe.*

*Here's the key*, he says.
*Go in, look for a false bottom*
*in the kitchen cupboard.*

*Before. Yes, the pantry. Whatever.*

*Directions in there for the safe house.*
*Might not look like it*
*at first, but that's what it is.*

*Before and then after. Sick.*

A day or two after, it was pretty obvious
the chemical attack they claimed
was really biological,

the clueless fucks – did they even know
the difference? – infections pulsing out
a week on from their release sites:
feral Venn diagrams.

Early days that summer,
people dropping like flies. Stupid,
then, of Kate, cute and stupid Katie, going out

to the vigil like that.
      Michaela tells me now,
someone spotted Kate, someone
in the group of shooters milling about
with cameras who recognised her – *From where*

*the fuck where?* – she said she didn't know.
A bug in the spooks,
      maybe. They marked her up

for when the guns came out.
                              I don't want to think about it.
I punched her hard in the face.
She had to've known
                    and didn't tell.

I am done.
I don't know where she is now
or what they did.


*Before. Politics.*

Wrecking everything
to make the conditions
suit you:

like creating a market
for what you're selling.


*After.*

Kwashiorkor


*After. Birds.*

The cockatoo – sulphur-crested –
drops from the tree, fixes me

with that grinning eye, says
*Nevermore.* I'm speechless. Ha.
*Yeah*, says Finn. *He's mine.*

*Say hello, Charlie.*

*Hello, Charlie*, he croaks.

Ha.
Ha.

*After. How we get bacon now.*

*Do him, and then
in with the pigs,*
he said, not
breaking eye contact.

Now he knows.
This guy's face blanks up,
maybe understanding.

He shouldn't have touched
those kids, he knew better,
surely.

*Before. Tag.*

Didn't quite see it clearly –
could've been HEER

but it looked a lot like HEED.


*Before. Happy birthday.*

*Happy birthday, darl,* mum
says, too close.
        I recognise
the smell of her breath,
but don't know,
though I try to find out,
what it's of.
        *Happy birthday*
*to you,* she croaks, as my little
spatter of friends and some
of their mums and someone's,
I think it must be, dad, them all
singing, wandering across
the key, dad's on the dogshift,
and all week, it's his turn, and
mum, as I'm blowing through
the hot sheet of seven candles,
staggers, sudden as if
hit,
    and rights herself a bit,
expertly, and I realise

with a start I never notice
she does that, it's just
part of her gait, her body
and how it moves, how she
moves it, but no-one else
does it, not that I ever see.
*Make a wish*, Nichelle's mum
sings,
  beaming at me
     as if
there was something wrong.
and was trying to make up for it
without it looking like that.
So I did.


*Before.*

I said to him, *No, but thanks.*

Not sure if that was shrewd.
Or shrewish.
Where do they meet?


*Before. Worst.*

He never would go down on me
with anything resembling conviction.

*Before. Mum, thinking.*

It went, and quick with it,
her mind. Her memory,
everything, it turns out,
as I see it, 's memory.
It never was that great,
with the drinking, probably,
after dad went, sick
of it all, but those last years,
(did you see much of her,
then?), it wasn't just that
she forgot – *what* she forgot:
stopped denying some of what
had happened. For years

closed me down, her fucking
mad bluster of *no*s.
                        Just shut
the fuck up, mum.
                        And then
suddenly she forgets –
forgets what was,
forgets to eat, to clean herself
up, and soils herself,
regresses back to nappies,
needs looking after –
not the baby I wanted.
How convenient for her.
Ridiculous I care at all, or
whatever it is I even feel.

*Before. Public transport.*

Cracks open the Beam and Coke,
feet up on the seat, visibly not caring.
*Cheers, up yours,* to the fines notice fraying,
amended.
            Grins, breathing on the ticket guy,
looking him up, looking him down –

the boy out of Cessnock, but.
All 60 kilos of him,
            if that.


*Before. Dreaming a boy.*

Here he is, fifteen, strutting
almost, on his own (I'm eyeing
him from a block behind,
trailing him, my red tartan skirt's
the hottest thing I can imagine
on a girl, not short enough,
but, and his boxed redheads
are deep in his pockets, in his
jeans, the frayed black ones
he wears, or in his jacket, tucked, I
reckon, in the inside pockets,
watching for the moment
he thinks no eyes are on him –
down the back lanes, the quiet
streets old people live on,
spitting, and spitting out

matches, flicking his thumb
across the box's strip, a
tearing sound and a stripe
of smoke, bouncing
lifeless off fences, dripping
into damp grass, into greenery
too moist to catch, and he's
so shy.
      We haven't
even pashed yet, but
oh shit yes I want to, not even knowing if.


*Before. Why Amy and Sam?*

*Debt, maybe*, he said. *Or the cancer.*
*Cheating, maybe. Maybe*
*he was cheating. Or she*
*was.* Went quiet, constructing
a slow frown almost. A furrow.
*I don't really know, sweet.*
*But I can guess. But I don't*
*really want to.*
           *Why do you*
*want to know?*
           I want to say,
*Because, dad, I fancied*
*the shit out of her.*
*I watched the two*
*of them at it in their yard*
*one night. I was a sudden*
*bomb of heat. That did*

*something to me;*
*it was something I knew*
*then that I wanted. But*
*who from.* But I don't.
*There's any number*
*of reasons someone*
*does that.* Him again.
A gif loops
in my mind – that arse
of hers, in those unnecessary
jodhpurs, how it swam.
She was face-down
in that weedy bottom dam.
They found him treading water
in the windy rafters.


*After. Found.*


The wound on his torso,
sun-stretched knife cut,
the shape of the swirl
on a drink can.


*Before. The river, with Kate.*


Crossing the Hunter
at Morpeth – the still river's
surface is a sheet of dewy glass,
laid down in the cool long paspalum,

and everything, or anything
moving across it — the birds, the high,
thin clouds, vapour trails, our walking
bodies twinned with hurrying want,
the ashy leaves dropping in only to float,
motionless — nothing leaves a trace there:
the dew melts away not quite noticeably:
only the deep smudge of what's underneath
stays, though what you see depends,
and grit, silt, litter, probably film it over.


*After. Cricket pfft.*

He told me (dad),
trying to school me
in the ways of cricket
as he understood them,

> *The aim of bowling leg spin,*
> *Miss Edwards, is to induce an error*
> *from your opponent.*

Before that,
nothing'd made sense.

So, obviously,
I filed that one away.

*Before. A sign.*

STOP
TORTURING
THEM
YOU
SICK
FUCKS


*Before. Ants' nests.*

Strung around the rim
of the showground, ideal habitat –

meniscus of shallow graves.


*Before. Dissent.*

Little bookish me
alone on the night train
                    again.
Him standing over
me, leery, pissy, mates
two-deep, them blushing
but curious – *Books, who*
*reads books. Losers*
*read books. William Gibson,*
*ooh, William. Poof's name.*
His mates mumble out their

blushing and *Come on, mate.*
He's not little but I put
down the book, author photo up,
so Bill can see, stand, coiled,
furious with everything my life is
or isn't,
              and I kick this guy, hard,
in the cunt
              And again, again.
His grinning mates back off, too.
I want to go full Arya Stark.
Next stop, Beresfield.

*After. His room.*

Cleaning it out, because of.
Next to Angela Carter, *Heroes and Villains,*
*The Hunger Games* set, in a nice slipcase.
Thumb-smudged all over the margins.

Remember all those dystopian novels
after COVID? –
how cute were they.

*After. Practice Wellness. The LOLZ.*

Here I am,
examining
the nature

of my anger,
the depth of
my resentment.
It's been
a long day
all morning.
I look around,
sniff at the air –
the wind's shifted,
a little –
so look around
again. What's
changed?
          The rounded shadow
my head makes
across my thinning
hand as it passes.
There is a pulse there,
still.
          I almost see it.


*Before. Promo.*

The coal lobbyist filmed
gesticulating vividly about the industry,
its future – slides off the edge
of the open cut at Bulga.

*Before. Rush hour.*

He was eating a pork roll right in my face.
Outside, the oleanders were in bloom.


*After. I'm asking for a friend.*

How do you think I feel about how I feel?


*After. Click.*

New ground, game trails. Three of us,
single file, spaced out, staggered.
Unless you were patient,
you'd see only one of us, and think,

                        *Yep, too easy.*
A small bend in the trail and a fuzzy
sudden whisper, a whirr. Is that
a click? So freeze.
               And again, once
I move. Snagged in *déjà vu.*
                   A sweaty look
around:
        a box suspended from the elbow
of that tree, winks when I move, and the sound with it.
Shimmy up.
          We get back, check it.
Shots of pademelon, quolls, dogs,
no foxes anywhere. Recent date stamps

on pics of compact shadows.
Not the month we thought it was.
Peeling sticker: *Property of Devil Ark.*


*After. Divine handmaid.*

I bet that opinionista
was less than ecstatic
living in the state
she wished upon others.


*Before. Ruthie's hair.*

Grass like her sun-bleached tips
we couldn't bear, that
short spring, to cut.


*After. Their evac.*

Someone ripped down,
burnt, shredded the road signs
from the freeway mid-evac –

but only the ones they were looking at
on their way, panicking out away
from the bugs and bombs.

They'd done a shit job.
Tearing out, west and up
through the Putty from memory

as Sydney was cracking up mid-conference,
I was constant, eyeing the wing mirror
for the darkened names of receding streets,

of overpasses, of behind.


*Before.*

The phone buzzing woke me.
*It's on*, he mutters, half-hoarse.
*Be there.* Whispering self-conscious,
even though he's in the car on his own
the wait just about over.
I'm out, a block off, waiting
away from the corners, and then,
by pre-dawn logic, here we are.
the plotted carpark skirts around
the small fibro hall.
                Another car
draws in, lights off, hissing slowly
like an opened can.
                Draws up, parallel,
windows down, a cliché from cop shows.
*It's fucken on.*
           Oh, shit.

*After. Process.*

Flies, beetles, bacteria
dismantle the fox.


*Before. Fuel to burn.*

I said the right things
in those close fibro rooms
and nervy pubs they met in.

Kate. Ridley said nothing about her,
they might not even have known
I was somebody's bait.

When they whinged about bitches,
I had to concur. If they knew, they'd've
cut me. Droning on about *lefties*

and proper protocol for the salute:
impenetrably deep, shallow as a reflection.
Here we are —
        GOOD FORTUNE Co.,
MIGRATION AGENTS.
                We mask up,
the bell above the frosted glass
door tinkles and I want to run
or to shit myself.

*After. Curtains.*

Distant thunder muffles
the flicker and billow
of late arvo's smoky light
at the kitchen's slow
yellow floral curtains.


*After. Choice.*

*Ditches for bitches,*
I heard one of them say,
those bald dudes
with the head tattoos,
before I shot the four of them.
Injudicious, I know, but
satisfying.
          Sailed on out of there
like a motherfucker, like some queen.


*After. A grave situation.*

Get fucked will I dig my own hole.
What will you do if I don't.

*Before. Sign.*

NO TURNING FACILITY AT END OF ROAD


*After. Online.*

Slower than dial-up,
it was, but Dilton scammed us
onto the web,
                    which kept crashing.
The world
                    had just kept on going,
answering that question.
Seriously droppy, but we could
get snags of American TV –
a tragicom set in Oz, we never
caught the name, with Steve Irwin
played by Justin Timberlake.
                              So. Um, wow.


*After. Party.*

Not a single bottle
of decent red
or even a room
temp white.

All the last wine we found
was goons:
foiled again.

*After.*

Some days
everything
tastes of ants.


*Before. What.*

Her fingers move through my hair,
slow and gentle, a smile flares
in her mouth's, her face's corner.
What does she mean by that?
*What are you doing, Irene? Leave
her alone.*
        That's Dad.
A *tone* in his voice.


*Before. Debt recovery.*

It was so easy to find out
where Ridley was.
Went to an old mate's
of his place, and said,

*Look, you know how it is.
That cunt, he owes me
money.*
        So easy to find.
Tick.
        And so it begins.

*After. P.S., I don't love you.*

Postscripts cop out,
they're a salve, savlon
on an amputee.

*1984, The Handmaid's Tale* –
these stories left behind
for a maybe kinder world

to find.
   I don't find that
all that realistic now. Sorry.


*After. The long day.*

In the scavenged camp chairs
we sit, the sun's thin alloy
resting on the staked-up tomato bushes,
the rows of citrus trees there on that run
of higher ground where the edge
of the park was, the spud beds,
the black plastic sheathing strawberries.
Much further, the hills, a hard brow.
I never was a green thumb
but now I don't care, it's easy, easier.

*After. Sugar hit.*

I miss the fructose
in fruit toast.


*After. T-shirt on a corpse, Cessnock Road.*

OBEY

I'll have that, thanks.


*Before. Pete. Before anything else, nearly.*

They found a body, but it's not him again.
This is what I think happened.
What I think happened to him.

He walked into the bush, the woods.
It's not especially dark there, not
crammed-in with sun-hard twigs

near eye level, not slinking with the fierce,
jagged little animals. But it is night,
probably, the moon's there, a small

round jag of it. He'd say he's there
alone. He would've checked, he'd have
known to've checked. Waited, looked

around, lazily looked over his shoulder,
making to be assessing a tree or to listen
more closely to a bird, for the precise

location of a cicada. Of each cicada.
Somewhere in there there's a body
of water, not very big. A waterhole,

a dam left over from the mine or
the farmlet you could sometimes
see the lights of, on the back road through,

or a rain-filled gully, nothing you could fairly
call a creek.
             And so he walks, on his own.

He knows the way, knows his way around.
A sound of cars, but pretty way off,
where people go who don't have rooms

of their own to go to, but can get a car. But
this time, voices, a bit quiet but enough
to hear, and lights, torches. No, spotlights,

powerful things that rip into the dark.
Something bounding through the bush,
making it crackle, a heavy thing, in a panic,

a couple of them, a roo? Roos? Oh, but
the shouting, that can't be right.
It's open here, not anywhere really

to duck into, behind. Should he
be hiding? How can you know.
Voices dangle from the moving.

Light swoops, and a falling sound and
he doesn't quite catch what's said,
if there were actual words at all,

only the air leaving a chest,
spilled from the mouth. Men.
Boys. Muffled tearing maybe and soon

panting.
            He gets flat to the ground as he knows
what's being done and gives out a noise

when the light creams itself in front of him.
That's when they see him, clear and sudden,
the stiff ring of them.

                        There's a cinderblock
building over there, at the edge of that blunt
clearing, where the track comes close,

for the Scouts' retreat.
                        That, they use it
for shelter.

            This
is what I think could've happened.
You hear things, but we never heard.

But the others.
The stories in the papers, in the courts:
what went on in the boys' home

where mum always threatened to send him
in the fights that stopped when I was ten
and he was suddenly gone,

and only the briefest explaint.


*Before. Sleep.*

Helping you fall asleep that summer –
the aircon finally hits
the power bills – shit! –
tracing your name on your curled-up back –
Ruth Alice Ridley, then again your name
as if you were mine –
Ruth Alice Kelly, and over: Ruth Alice Kelly, Ruth Alice Kelly.
Ruth.
     Alice.
        Kelly.
And what if, really, you'd been mine, ours?
Who would you be then? Not that sick,
slick boy who didn't quite make it.
Your cousin.
        Our blue little boy.
So little. Who we wanted after,
only after we couldn't keep you.
Who would you've been,
        then?

*After. Ember in my hair.*

Fingers in my hair,
her mouth warm and close,
open and slick:
*Bit of grey here, looks*
*like.*
      Hand at my chest.
Later the mirror confirms
it: a long strand turning
silver, a wave in it that fits,
almost, the curve of my breasts.
In this crappy mirror
it's a discovery like the glint
of water below that ridge
in the dry grey bush before
that stash of maps –
                  that thick wad
rustled up from the library.
I added bits to their wide spread,
taping on pages past the limits,
drawing in the view from high
ground, annotating like the outlines
of town or home or our yard
I'd scribble as a kid.

            My hair keeps
turning. Michaela saw it too,
says, *You look like mum only*
*shorter. But longer hair.*
*And not such a fucken cow. Not completely.*

After the sunshower's passed,
pale strands of light
                    dangle
from the damp candlebarks.
I wake, groggy, it's still light.
Is she still here? I don't remember.

That shoulder, it's still sore.


*After. The bees.*

I'd never seen so many bees before
Where had they returned from?
At first – the buzz – I'd assumed
piles of corpses or something,
and a tent of blue flies on each one
the air glistening with its spill of maggots –
but this sweet and potent smell
instead, with smoke in it,
                            way off.


*Before.*

*I'm good to you, ya dopey bitch,*
*because ya need me to be.*

What mum said to her. Years
and years back

*Your sister? She's fine. Just fine.*

Mum, I was never 'fine'.


*Before. T-shirts, couples.*

Him in his black Vernon Ah Kee:
    *australia*
    *driveit*
    *likeyou*
    *stole it*

She's wearing Buzzcocks.
*Ever fallen in love?*


*Before.*

In the vestibule
a thin man in the same
shirt as me.


*After.*

DO NOT
QUEUE ACROSS
INTERSECTION

smothered with burnt out cars

*Before.*

Near Rookwood
a ghost hoarding
a narrow space between walls –

WE SAVED SYDNEY'S HERITAGE


*After. An ideal home.*

Melton Avenue. Warm tarmac glugs
up in summer so we use the footpaths.
Away from the drains, but not so far.
This empire of weatherboards, dusty
block after block. Thin veneers of paint
come off with your fingers if you touch.
Wild, they'd gone, the fruit trees,
this neck of town. Cut them right back,
prune the shit out of them until now –
that fresh hard smell, sweet, the tang
I'd barely remembered, it'd seemed
lost, and utterly, like your face, Little Love,
like your voice, our whole family of three.
They fill our tubs now, we trade them.
Selling: that's gone. What did money
ever even feel like.

*Before. The candidate.*

She comes across as a kind of mid-range Ayn Rand.


*Before. The other candidate.*

He comes across as threatening wallpaper,
all mouth, no trouser.


*After. In lieu of the loo.*

does anyone
come here to
play with there
cocks ifso when??

yeah 7am

Abermain War Memorial mens –
the ladies' porcelain jagged as shark teeth

*Before.*

Quiet Wednesday afternoon.
Just into autumn, the first
properly cold days, the scraping wind.
Going through her secret stash
in the back sunroom.
*Dad? You here?* though he'd gone,
weeks before, finished with her
at last. But the smell of him
somewhere, maybe?
                    Ancient clutter
of mogadon, serepax, xanax.
Others. Zoloft. Naltrexone. The script on some
faded, not all of them in her name,
though the foil's still bright, fresh lead
snapped in the sun.
                    Pull the curtain aside,
that cracking plastic on that loose cable.
Those fucking hideous roses,
tight and interlocked, pink, yellow
on pale blue. Or is it mauve?
The glass needs a wipe, a hose down.
Enclosed by my face's dim reflection,
still and sudden – something long
and slightly swaying in the lilly pilly.

*Before. Do something.*

I could go to the media about him. Them.
But what would the *Cessnock Advertiser* do?
The *Maitland Mercury*?


*Just. Before.*

Did you see that video the kid shot
from his balcony, waving at first to his mum,
her all waves and smiles,

it's cute, she's just going to the shop
across the street for milk and a surprise,
and then a sudden high clapping

and she falls in the road.
                    The three men
reflector sunnies, not masks, though
everyone remembers masks.


                  The kid
must've frozen, panicked. They cross the road,
out of shot, blocked by the balcony
then the sound of a door giving way.

Who released it?
                  Who'd want it released?

*After. Down and then out the quick way.*

Miles out from the Tops,
a long hard scrabble down –
scaling it must've been
a shit. *Short cut*, M says.

I know her deal. She
knows me too well – all I
can do is keep eyes
on the rock face, the iron hue,

the red in the sandstone my breath
lights on, the rocks almost
yellow, jaundiced.
                              A tall
fence at the bottom,

spiked with barbed wire,
razor wire, all *ad hoc*. Probably
was.
            An old cut in the wire –
pulled back like a scab. Just past

there, a thatch of clothing,
slashed in the weather, the
cascading wind, the tearing
rain, and then flaps of skin out

from the faded winter gear,
and hair nearly the colour
of Ruth's, maybe a shade or two
lighter, all of the mess hissing

streaming snagged up and from
the impossible wire, the fence
she dropped on.
              Michaela won't
look but doesn't exactly

hurry past. Then a quick
glance back, sly, over
her shoulder. If I didn't know
her, I'd say it was rueful.

Away then into damper
understorey, leeches onto
our blood. But somewhere
near to the fringes, we must

be – kookaburras hacking
up their laughter, and cockatoos,
being cockatoos, circling up there
white against the blue.


*Burying the jars. After.*

This soft soil.
These hard hands,
fingers like forks
plunging into the dirt.
Fold the sheets
into these dusty jars.
Seal the lid.
What else

am I going to do
with them?
It's warm here,

        too warm.


*Before.*


And so that's how I came to turn so hard and so sweet.


*First night, that night. Voices.*


The gunshots.
Oh fuck, get down
into the warm dark under.
Voices at the door.
Coughs, a hacky sounding sort
of cough.
        *Kel, Kel,* one calls out
after mumbles, deciding
on the plan, not
having made one before.
              *Where
are you? There's. Something's
happening, Kel.*
Stomping that's trying not
to panic, feet wanting to run.
*Nup, she's not here, mate.*

His voice.
*How can you tell,*
a statement, no query
in that blankness.
                    *Just trust me.*
Must've given him a look.
*Always leaves her phone*
*in the fucken kitchen.*
                    *Not here.*
*Call her then, make very*
*fucking sure.*


          In my arse pocket,
on vibrate and straight to voicemail.
*Not a sound*, the other one says. *Where*
*fucking is she?*
*Musta gone out. Or run.*
                    *Kel,*
*if you're here, we find you.*


*Know what you done, Kel, who*
*ya talked to, don't we, Rids.*
*We know now.*
Sounds for a while from a thorough search.
Thorough enough for him, I suppose.




*Before and then after. Labels.*


Who was doing this killing,
so methodical, the bodies —
wrote their names on the feet,

their legs, with sharpies.
The headshots, the disintegrated
faces, but they must've wanted
the names of the dead known
and put about. But less effective
once the web went down,
the power off at the switch.
I never recognised the names,
not for sure, but I read them all,
in case,
        and wrote them down.
They're here, somewhere, page
after page after page.


*After. New.*

One last smell
of her pillow,

and I'm gone.


*Before. Go.*

*Go go go*
I want to tell her,
that lady in the clip.
*Just go.*
        There's still time,
isn't there?

# Notes

The line on page 13, "Things looked bad", quotes Michael Dransfield.

"You're my only friend,/ You don't even like me."
Many thanks to Joel Silbersher for his kind permission to reproduce the lyric from "My pal", by God.

"thanks, / thanks a lot": borrowed from John Forbes, "Europe, Endless", *Damaged Glamour*.

The lines "The first time/ ever I saw your face" reference the Ewan MacColl song of the same name.

# Acknowledgements

This book, set primarily on unceded Wonnarua and Darkinjung Country, was written mostly on and while crossing Darug and Gandagarra Country. I pay my respect to their Elders past, present and future.

The cover image is a detail from the 1977. Cessnock 1:50 000 topographic map. Record 9132-2. Geoscience Australia, Canberra. (http://pid. geoscience.gov.au/dataset/ga/57915) . It is used under the Creative Commons Attribution 4.0 International Licence.

Some sections of *camping underground* were previously published in *Cordite*. Thanks to Nathan Curnow, the guest editor, and to Kent McCarter, editor of *Cordite*. Thanks also to Toby Fitch for the invitation to the Poetry Night at Sappho in 2017 where I read early sections of this book.

I'm in the debt of readers of early versions of this book for their support, questioning and feedback: Inez Brewer, Bonny Cassidy, Erin Gough, Will Hilton, David Prater and Michelle Weisz.

Many thanks to David Musgrave and everyone at Puncher & Wattmann for their support in getting *camping underground* out. My thanks also to Ross Gillett for his careful reading and edit of a late version of the manuscript, and to Morgan Arnett for typesetting this beast of a thing.

My gratitude to Pam Brown, Fiona McFarlane, Toby Fitch and John Hughes for their kind words in support of this book.

This book is for Inez and Frankie.

www.ingramcontent.com/pod-product-compliance
Lightning Source LLC
Chambersburg PA
CBHW030830090426
42737CB00009B/947